NO GOD NEXT DOOR

RED RULE IN MEXICO
AND OUR RESPONSIBILITY

BY

MICHAEL KENNY, S. J., Ph. D., Litt. D.

Author of "Romance of The Floridas",
"The Mexican Crisis", etc., etc.

WILLIAM J. HIRTEN CO., Inc.

25 BARCLAY STREET

NEW YORK

MEXICAN CALVARY

This I have seen:
             a nation hung
On its bleeding cross, with arms outflung
   To sever the startled air of dawn
   As out of the night is Calvary born;
And the Rio crimsons beneath the tide
Of blood that flows from the crucified,
   Whilst the Christ once slain in the long ago
   Has mounted a cross in Mexico.

This have I heard:
             a people's cry
As strong men weep and brave men die,
And deep is the warning, the message shown
   When brave men sicken and strong men moan;
Four hundred years are looking down
On a shattered breast and a martyr's crown,
   Where a rifle shot was the warning bell
   For the clash of truth with the spawn of hell.

This do I know:
             a brother bleeds
On a neighboring strand, where choking weeds
   Have felled the young in a reeking mire.
   An Indian church is wreathed in fire—
From under arches, broken, burned
A nation's eyes to a nation turned
   Bespeak their challenge, hope, regret—
   Quicken us Lord!—lest we forget.

                      A. R. McGratty, S. J.

Foreword

Archbishop's Residence
San Antonio, Texas.

July 19, 1935.

I hail with genuine delight the appearance of "No God Next Door." May it be an eye-opener for our American people.

Too many of our easy going, good-natured fellow citizens look upon the doings across the Rio Grande with an amused, incredulous eye, Yet one must be blind not to detect the intense menace to our own free institutions, to our democracy and liberty, in the Calles and Cardenas policies, as well as their destruction of religion and all liberties in Mexico.

Moscow has its laboratory, its efficient workshop in Mexico. And it is not merely distracted Mexico they want to conquer; they are after bigger game. The Colossus, our own United States, is what they wish to bag in their relentness war against God and Christian civilization. They have actually established in this City of San Antonio the first "cell" for Communist propaganda in the United States; and I know personally of astounding perversions amongst our young people who have become enthusiastic propagandists of the Stalin and Lenin philosophies with their atheism and communism.

The need of American enlightenment and action is even more pressing now than under Calles.

Against his own law. Cardenas is forcing atheistic education on the Universities; and his decree confiscating all properties that are even suspected of any connection with religion at any time, and offering state reward for informers thereof, is the most effective device for rooting out priests, sacraments, and religion that history records. Unable to risk the ruin of homes by seeking religious shelter or extending it, priests and people are holding out despairing hands to us to withhold our rulers from support of the diabolic tyrants of Mexico.

May "No God Next Door" be read by many. Our leaders, lay and cleric, our diocesan and national organizations, the Knights of Columbus and Holy Name, and our men and women societies, our sodalities and schools and colleges and press, should strive to put this book in the hands of every American citizen.

It comes at the timeliest moment to enlighten our people on this deadlier than all the persecutions we have denounced in other lands and to impel them to demand and exact that our Government give Mexico a new deal in American justice. May it also be the saving antidote for not a few of our Americans already tainted with the virus that comes to us via Mexico and Russia.

☒ ARTHUR J. DROSSAERTS,
Archbishop of San Antonio

Author's Acknowledgements

The writer would record his indebtedness for the inspiration furnished by **Father Miguel Agustin Pro** and the many heroic martyrs of Mexico, to whom he dedicates this story of a long-suffering Christian people.

He would also make grateful acknowledgement to V. Rev. J. M. Walsh, S. J. his New Orleans Provincial, who authorized his researches, and to his Excellency Archbishop Curley, who had their record published in **The Baltimore Review**; to the noble men and women in Mexico, who supplied him, at much risk, with ample material for his findings; and to the men and women of all classes whose heroic sacrifice and religious loyalty it was his privilege to witness. Among these he would mention: the faithful Indians who wove so cunningly a carpet of multi-colored flowers for Our Lady of Guadalupe Shrine that he mistook it for a huge Persian rug and who by faithful worship in their ravished churches atoned for such sacrilege; the tradesmen and peasants who set up altars in their shops and homes when their churches were robbed of them; the children who sang out bravely in chorus, Hay Dios, Hay Dios when taught that God is not; the student delegates of twenty-four Universities who risked their careers by training for a week in Mexico City under Jesuit guidance to preserve their nation's institutions from the atheo-communist taint; the Catholic leaders of National Defense who daily challenge death for liberty; the two thousand priests who, often in penury and rags and hunted as felons, still bring the bread of Christ to their people; and the two-hundred Jesuits, all native Mexicans and all under ban, but all there organizing young and old, parents and sodalities, students and teachers, workers and merchants, employers and employees, issuing and distributing varied and apposite literature to keep the Faith in Mexico, and presenting other proofs that in multiple sacrificial activity and in sterling patriotic as well as religious devotedness, there is no Jesuit body in the world superior to the Jesuits of Mexico nor truer to the ideals of Ignatius Loyola.

Altogether, our people may take the message confidently to heart.

The author takes occasion of the second printing to express his gratitude for the numerous commendations that helped quickly to dispose of the large first edition, and particularly for the highly commendatory letters with which he has been honored by the Father General of his Order, by the Chairman of the Mexican Bishop's Committee, by Archbishop Pizzardo, Secretary to the Vatican for Extraordinary Ecclesiastical Affairs, and through him by the words of the Holy Father himself, blessing this little book and suggesting diffusion of its contents through the European press.

THE CATHOLICS OF MEXICO ARE BRETHREN WORTH PRAYING FOR, AND WORKING FOR, AND FIGHTING FOR.

Contents

CHAPTER I

THE CALLES PLAN TO CAPTURE CONSCIENCES
Viewed By Canabal and Mr. Daniels

"RUSSIA on the Rio Grande" and "Our Bolshevist Border" first sprung to mind as proper captions for a frank description of Mexican Government today.

Soon, however, these were found inadequate to picture an administrative system more ruthlessly planned and executed and in most important essentials more destructive of law and liberty and every elemental right, human and divine, than the reddest and rawest that Lenin and Stalin have so far inflicted on humanity. Nor would any title be adequate that ignores our share in this development.

This statement was written at El Paso, within a hundred yards of the Mexican border. The writer has been through Mexico's highways and has made a twenty-year study of its highwaymen; and he is ready to substantiate his settled conviction that the one ruling power in this round world today that is most diametrically and consciously antagonistic to the whole course of Christian civilization and to the principles and practices of the United States Government and system, is the Government that now rules with

a rod of iron on the other side of the Rio Grande.
He might further state that this iron rod is laid
with systematic mercilessness on the back of
liberty, by the grace and favor, however uncon-
scious, of the United States.

Calles Lauds Tabasco's Anti-Christ

For over a decade the ruling power, actual and
absolute, no matter who held title, has been
Plutarco Elias Calles. All presidents and governors and party leaders called him "El Jefe
Maximo," the Chief Supreme, with trembling
awe. He was Hitler and Stalin combined, but
more resolute and practical in actuating the worst
aims of either. He set up and upset cabinets and
ministers at will, and made and kept every president his puppet and every governor his mouthpiece. This is axiomatic with friends and foes
alike in Mexico, who are equally aware that
Calles and all Government were synonyms. They
only differ in calling it, the one a Republic,
Socialist, Communist, or Revolutionary; the
other an absolute autocratic tyranny.

It should be noted here that the recent fall of
Calles, whether temporary or permanent, marks
no change in anti-Christian policy, for Portes
Gil, the new head of the Revolutionary Party,
has all the Calles bias against religion, and Cardenas is a more thorough and consistent Communist than either.

On what supreme aim did Calles concentrate
this absolute supremacy of power? What was
his dominating purpose? This he has never left
in doubt. He proclaimed it before the so-called
election of his creature Cardenas and while laud-

ing its most perfect executor in Tabasco, Governor Garrido Canabal, who has exemplified sexual education with a naked simplicity that the rudest savages never reached.

To Universalize De-Christianizing Teachings

But the gratifying actuation of his plan in Tabasco and Sonora and other States, whose governors were quickest and keenest to read the mind and win the favor of El Jefe, was not enough. His system must run in every State and place and home in Mexico, and dominate all minds from the cradle to the grave. With his growth in power the plan of his supreme purpose has grown in definiteness of aim and specification, and the Calles policy was never more definite than now.

Escorted by President Rodriguez and President-elect Cardenas, Governor Allende, and his other principal officials, "El Jefe Maximo de la Revolucion," the Calles title of supremacy, addressed, June 20, from the Governor's palace of Jalisco the entire people of Mexico. The revolution had been realized, he said, in the definite ideology of President Rodriguez and his similarly ideologic successor Cardenas, but it has yet to be completed and made permanent in the psychological period which the Revolution has now entered; and this is how:

"We must enter into consciences and take possession of them: the conscience of the children and the conscience of the youth; for the youth and the child must belong to the Revolution.

"It is absolutely necessary to drag the enemy

out of his trench. The Conservatives are the enemy; and their trench is education, their trench is the school. It would be a grave and cowardly dereliction of duty not to snatch our youth from the claws of the clericals, from the claws of the conservatives; and unfortunately the schools in many States and in the Capital are directed by the clerical and reactionary elements.

"We cannot leave the future of the country, the future of the revolution in enemy hands. With all their trickery the clericals cry: 'The child belongs to the home; the youth belongs to the family.' Egoistic doctrine! Child and Youth belong to the Community, to the collective body; and it is the revolution's inescapable duty to attack this section, and dispossess them of consciences, to uproot all prejudices (i.e., religious beliefs) and to form a new national soul.

"For this end I urge and exhort all the governments of the republic, all the authorities of the republic, all the revolutionary elements of the republic, that we give definite battle, on whatsoever plane and to whatsoever limit, in order that the consciences of the youth shall belong to the Revolution."

Applying Moscow's Atheizing Methods

Calles' statement that the Church still controlled many schools was false. There was not one Catholic or Christian school of any class in Mexico that his government had not suppressed, or transformed into a paganizing medium. It is true that the universities had rebelled against Bassols, his minister of education, who was forcing his system upon them, and fathers and mothers of families had made organized protest against his method of executing that system in the primary schools. This method, copied from Moscow and transplanted by Governor Garrido Canabal of Tabasco, whom Calles singled out for special eulogy, explains what he means by "taking possession of consciences."

Education must be socialistic and scientific, and hence must be directed against all religion and its practices, which are denounced as degrading superstitions; and social relations, which are based upon sex, must be exemplified scientifically. Hence religious symbols were replaced by pictures caricaturing the Crucifixion and the Mass and the religious truths and services traditionally sacred; and for scientific exposition of social relations boys and girls were stripped naked in the schools to see with their own eyes the facts of sex. Even animals were exhibited in further illustration, and systematized brutish and blasphemous devices were utilized to demonstrate that the child was merely a brute, and to extirpate God and religion and reverence and Christian law and morals from the mind and heart of Mexico.

Satanic Sacrifice of Souls

This is the meaning of Calles' dogma that the child and youth belong, not to the home and family, but to the Revolution; and this is his set method of forming "a new national soul." It is a sacrifice of souls as horrifying as the human holocausts the Aztecs offered to their idols. But the Calles' idol has also had such sacrifice; not only the countless victims of his last decade's de-Christianizing campaigns, but in his present paganizing school program.

Among the various representative delegations that dared to denounce the teachings and illustrative methods prescribed by his minister were four hundred mothers, many with babies in their arms. Bassols ordered his mounted police to disperse them by riding through their ranks, the charge resulting in numerous injuries and several fatalities. When, notwithstanding, a number of these brave Christian matrons forced their way to his office and began to voice their remonstrances, he turned on his radio at its loudest and dismissed them with contemptuous mockery.

Lessons in Lewdness Drive Victims Insane

So went brazenly on the Calles-Bassols process of making "a new national soul." Teachers unsympathetic or averse to the system were replaced by disciples of the Revolution, however unqualified educationally; and these, many of them ungrounded in the elements, qualified for favor and advancement in the degree of their zeal to inculcate blasphemy and sexual obscenity. They distributed, and still distribute, free tickets to the lewdest movies, the worst of the kind that stirred our American Legion of Decency to action; and, not content with object lessons in procreation, they took their pupils to maternity hospitals to witness parturition.

It was only when one of the girls who were thus outraged in all their instincts grew insane at the spectacle that the universal protests of parents, pupils, and people, and even the students of his own autonomous university, constrained Calles to replace Bassols by a less crude though equally "Red" revolutionary.

Conscience-killing Teachings Officially Extended

But its program continued in fact and in preachment, and the proclaimed determination to make it universal and so eradicate religion and Christian morality and form a new national soul on the Moscow plan became more and more pronounced. Accordingly, the new secretary of education, Eduardo Vasconcelos, issued promptly a general order prescribing for all schools the Calles rule and style of commandeering consciences. President-elect Cardenas has obediently echoed the Chief to the same effect, that there must be unity of conscience in the entire nation, and this the State must form by owning and controlling schools and youth, to the absolute exclusion of religionists and clericals. The Vasconcelos echo is more specific:

"As General Calles affirms, we must seize this psychologic period of spiritual conquest and take possession of the consciences of children and youth by the teachings in our schools. The Revolutionary party has proclaimed the State sole director of schools and teachers and teachings; and the Plan demands the exclusion of all religious teaching . . . replacing it by the interpretation of our revolutionary spirit," so as "to root out of the juvenile mind all sectarian and confessional prejudices."

How Canabal Qualified For Cabinet

The most brilliant executor of the Plan and the most highly commended by the Chief, its author, was and is Governor Garrido Canabal of Tabasco, later promoted to the Cabinet for his de-Christianizing services and now appointed by Cardenas Supreme Head of Education in Tabasco. Calles' son, Rodolfo, Governor of Sonora, had done very well, closing all churches and banishing all priests with the declared intention of introducing the Canabalesque culture of Tabasco and thus clamping his father's conscience plan upon schools. But the palm for design and execution of conscience-killing curricular devices belongs without challenge to Garrido Canabal. He has best applied the lessons which the specialists whom Calles had sent to study the Soviet educational system had brought back from Russia, for he possesses eminently the suitable aptitude of brutal fanaticism. He is, says **Omega,** of Mexico City, "classed with brute animals and has made himself one of them."

Literally so. At a cattle exposition, to which he summoned his officials and all the public school children, he exhibited bulls, cows, stallions, boars, etc., in action, naming the prize bull "God," and the prize animals in each class by other sacred titles. Reserving a great Spanish ass for special baptism with music and mock religious ceremony, Garrido Canabal himself baptized him "Pope," and having escorted the donkey in solemn procession through the streets, enthroned him in the Governor's palace. The many who pronounce him "Cannibal" deemed it an insult to the ass; "demoniac" would be more descriptive. Incredible as they seem, these and other even more shocking devices to implement the Calles atheizing plan may be verified in

Excelsior, Palabra, Universal, La Prensa, El Hombre Libre, and the general Mexican press.

Bans Christian Signs As Well As Morals

He had, by autocratic decree, abolished the place-names of God and of Saints and of varied religious import that hallow the lakes and streams and hills and towns and streets of Mexico; and the character of his deforming replacements for the geographic nomenclature of the whole state may be gathered from the names he inflicted on his own sons: Lenin, Lucifer and Satan. His anti-Christian fanaticism extended even to the graveyards. Enraged by the sight of Crosses and Christian signs on monuments and sepulchres and even the Christian names inscribed on the slabs, he had them all torn down or obliterated, and he issued peremptory order to every town and village that no tombstone in Tabasco have cross or script, and that numbers only should be used to identify the dead. Whether because it recalls his many victims or implies the immortality of the soul, an outlawed dogma, he has also abolished mourning; and so, black is taboo in Tabasco, a taboo adopted by several governors of like trend, even in Mexico City.

Searing The Souls Of Children

But the Garrido Canabal mentality has been most active in the schools. Taking hints from Moscow, he had the classrooms adorned with such pictures as a monk and a nun in lustful approaches eagerly disrobing; and he has issued an illustrated educational treatise, which he had his legislature endorse, September 16, 1933. This hyper-Bolshevist curio presents: "The mental purification by the teachers of the workers' belief in religious dogmas and divinities that do not exist," as symbolized by a group of workers pouring alcohol into the Grijalva river; for Garrido Canabal is a fanatic prohibitionist, in theory. The workers do not seem enthusiastic; but he assures us that "having lived eight years without priests or churches or religious practices, they are now flourishing in economic prosperity and culture under the dictates of reason."

They do not look it; yet, he tells us, "having ceased to appeal to their Gods for the justice that criminal egoisms denied them, they are now convinced their emancipation lies in themselves." These as well as the actors in all his pictured dramas have been forcibly imported for the setting.

He next presents an ancient church of striking beauty, which he has perverted into a school where "the sterile art and gloomy literature of the clerics" are replaced by "libertarian" luminants. This is typical of the thousands of fine churches these licentious Communists have seized and profaned.

Christ and Calvary Burlesqued

Pictures follow of children and youths gathered on the national feast of Our Lady of Guadalupe to witness the burning of "miraculous images and other religious fetiches, the last remnant of an obscurantism and ignominy that has passed." Other "fetiches," including a long venerated Crucifix and a Miraculous Virgin, are desecrated and cast into the waters to "the de-

rision of the populace"; but neither actors nor
spectators show signs of derision, looking more
like prisoners in line.

The illustrations culminate in a mock "Way of
the Cross" for Holy Week and a Crucifixion in
which the Magdalen is presented with a cigarette
in her mouth. Though she and most of the actors
look like sullen prisoners forced into a pose, their
improvisor, Garrido, offers them as proof of the
"mental evolution of the workers and their contempt for the practices by which the priests de-
ceived humanity."

These mockeries of the most sacred religious
sanctities, beliefs and practices were set to music
furnished by Governor Garrido Canabal's own
band; and he informs his complacent legislators
that he has established a socialist-communist
center for the diffusion of art, literature, music,
and song calculated to "defanaticize" the minds
of the masses not only in Tabasco but through all
the States, with which he had established connections, and in the Capital itself. He has enriched the Tabascan folklore with melodies em-
bodying the object lessons of his sexual teachings, and besides much literature of like order,
he had enacted and distributed widely such dramas as "The Farces and Crimes of the Confessional." He was thus planting "the essential
teaching of the rationalistic school" in the mind
and heart of child and youth and worker, and, in
uprooting the "false and enslaving" beliefs and
practices of tradition, was laying secure foundations for a Socialist Communist State.

Calles Sanctions Canabal's Savageries

These fanatic ravings and abnormities might be ascribed to such upcastings of an hysterial revolutionary period as threw Robespierre and many like monsters to the surface, soon to sink back to obscurity without seriously affecting the movement or stamping it with their imprint. But not so Garrido Canabal. His acts and personality have been sealed with the high, formal, and authoritative approval of the nominal president and of the actual head and chief of the Mexican Republic for a decade.

Calles, at the height of his triumph in last year's "election" of his candidates, gave definite public approval to the character and deeds and the entire educational program and procedure of the Governor of Tabasco, and held him up as the flower of the revolution and the model of all governors. Moreover, so highly was he known to be valued by the High Chief, that Cardenas, who was given the whole electoral vote by Calles' direction, cast his own vote for Garrido Canabal as the most worthy candidate for the presidency of Mexico.

This was manifestly intended, and was accepted, as official proclamation from the Capital that the brutalities of his conscience-catching campaign in Tabasco, which gave him national notoriety, had won him fullest sanction from the High Chief and marked him up as exemplar to all Governors in prosecution of Calles' proclaimed educational purpose to rape and revolutionize consciences. This sanction by the supreme power of policies and practices that stunk in the nostrils of all decency was further heightened by the semi-official announcement that the worthy selected for the Secretaryship of Agriculture or of Education was this same Garrido Canabal. The fact that this sacrilegious brute soon entered the Cabinet, dominating every department, presents a complete picture of the rule that ruins Mexico.

Morrow Screens Calles' Murder of Martyrs

The papers were full of it, and also of the antics and outrages that had given Garrido Canabal malodorous notoriety, and even administration organs dared to manifest disgust. It was clear that the High Chief was resolved to Canabalize despotically all schools and consciences in Mexico; but it also became clear to Calles that he needed further backing to silence or ride down opposition. He got it how and where he had found it invariably before in every crisis imperilling his power. He was able to induce the highest representative of the United States Government and people to rush promptly and publicly to his rescue.

When, at first convenience, he had broken all his saving pacts with the Church to secure him suppression of the widespread and effective Cristero uprisings against his tyranny, and was slaying and despoiling the heroic fighters and their sympathizers, male and female, indiscriminately, he had Mr. Dwight Morrow ride with him through the land in evidence of American support of a policy that had just executed the saintly young priest, Father Miguel Pro and a host of other heroes pictured in Cuevas' **Historia**, Volume V. He even played Toreador in one of the rich ranches he had annexed to impress the Ambassador and us with his happy democracy.

Notables Lured to Cover Calles' Crimes

To further distract American attention from his treacherous anti-Christian campaign of assassinations and despoilments, he managed to secure the service of our popular Colonel Lindberg in picturesque flights over a prosperous pacified Mexico. Later he had the helpful publicity of the Lindberg tour in United States papers extended and enhanced by the calculated clownings over the same terrain of the likewise, though otherwise, popular Will Rogers, who wired pithy praises of Mexico's Government, substituting for what "I see in the papers" the observations he made from an airplane.

But the rising indignation against the Bassols-Canabal enormities and his own pronouncements in the recent elections, had again to be held under the ever-potent threat of official American support; and this, in the face of facts of public knowledge and of diplomatic proprieties, Calles was again able mysteriously to secure from the United States official representative.

The important assistance rendered to Calles by this American, or un-American, actor deserves a chapter for itself.

CHAPTER II

OUR AMBASSADOR AIDS CALLES' COMMUNISTS

ON July 25, 1934, Honorable Josephus Daniels, United States Ambassador to Mexico, addressed, at his Embassy, a group of tourist teachers from the United States, escorted by Mexican educators. He had ample means of knowing what precisely their Mexican education meant. The atheistic and demoralizing educational methods and purposes of Bassols and Canabal, and Calles' proclamation that these must be made universal and perpetual, were just then filling the newspapers and exciting indignant public attention. Moreover, widely quoted articles from the Canabal organ Redencion, explained what the State and Federal rural schools were effecting since the present Calles system got good momentum in 1929. It said in part:

"By a constructive educational program the Indians were made to realize that there exist no miracles except those achieved by human intelligence and labor . . . The incineration of crosses, images of saints, and all other implements of the Catholic cult, has shown magnificent results."

Ignorant of Jefferson

The implements employed in the Calles-Canabal schools for further uprooting religion and morality and reducing the Indians to worse than pre-Christian debasement, was also the subject of much comment by the press and, with special disgust, by the American colony. Yet, with all this presumably in mind, Mr. Daniels said solemnly to the American and Mexican educators and people:

"The spirit of Mexico today was clearly and succinctly expressed last week at Guadalajara, in a phrase as brief as Jefferson employed some decades ago. General Calles, directing all Mexican patriots and especially those exercising directive functions, said: 'We ought to enter into and take possession of the mind of the children, of the mind of the youth.' In order to realize this ideal, which is the only one that can give to Mexico the high place visioned for it by its statesmen, the Government has been making the rural schools a social institution."

It will be seen that, in view of his American audience, Mr. Daniels dexterously substituted "mind" for "conscience" as used by Calles. Then, launching fulsome praise of Secretary Vasconcelos' report of rural schools, while noting not at all the dereligionizing aim and plan set forth in that document, Mr. Daniels continued:

"General Calles has seen, like Jefferson, that no people can be at the same time ignorant and free. For the same reason he, and President Rodriguez, and the President-elect Cardenas, and all the statesmen of ample vision, have been establishing education as the principal duty of the country. They recognize that General Calles has launched a challenge that goes to the root of the settlement of all problems of tomorrow when he said: 'We must enter into and take possession of the mind of the children, of the mind of the young.' "

Thus has our ambassador poured eulogy, fulsome and unqualified, on an educational system that not only denies religious liberty, but is expressly constructed and implemented in order to root out religion itself, and to establish in its stead a materialist, Communist, atheistic state, directly the opposite of the country he represents. Quite correctly he singles for preeminence the mind and will that molds and drives that program, linking with Calles the presidential puppets in whose name he operated his tyranny, but unhappily linking also with him and his measures the prestige and the principles of the United States and its religious and civil liberty.

Daniels Puts Calles on Par With Jefferson

His bracketing of Jefferson with Calles might be termed a diplomatic blasphemy as well as blunder. He surely should have known that it was Thomas Jefferson's influence that secured the First Amendment to our Constitution: "Congress shall make no law respecting an establishment of religion or prohibiting the free exercise thereof"; and that it was the same Jefferson who extended this principle in wider and clearer form to our every law-making body for all time. It was he who drew up the 1787 Ordinance, unanimously adopted by our First Congress: "To fix and establish the fundamental principles of religious liberty as the basis of all laws, Constitutions, and

Governments which forever after shall be
formed." Of the Six Articles of Compact ordained
for this purpose between each State and the Federal Government, the first provides that no peac-
able person "shall ever be molested on account
of his mode of worship or religious sentiments";
and the Third Article reads: **"Religion, Morality,
and Knowledge being necessary for good government and the happiness of mankind, schools and
the means of education shall forever be encouraged."**

This was a requisite part of the enabling laws
admitting to the Union every State thereafter;
and thus has Jefferson set in our Constitutional
basis the religion and morality which the Calles
system specifically and virulently proscribes.
Thus also does he specify that the schools to be
encouraged should impart religious and moral
knowledge, and that ignorance of this is incom-
patible with liberty and happiness. The schools
which the Ambassador of his presidential successor commends in his name are definitively and
purposively the reverse, distinctly promotive of
that ignorance which Jefferson held destructive
of good government and freedom.

Perhaps not much knowledge of constitutional
foundations should be expected of a politician
who mounted to high office by the ladder of partisan service; but a former cabinet officer and
present Ambassador should be cognizant at least
of Washington's farewell warning to our people
on this subject: **"It is substantially true that virtue and morality is a necessary spring of popular
government. . . . Reason and experience both for-**

bid us to expect that national morality can prevail in exclusion of religious principle."

Yet the notoriously fanatic exclusion of religious principle, and of the morality that reason and all human experience prescribe, from the rural and all other schools in Mexico, did not deter our Ambassador from strengthening them, as far as he might, with United States sanction.

It has been urged that if Ambassador Daniels has spoken in ignorance of such conditions he should be recalled as unfit for his trust, and if cognizant he should be dismissed for betraying it. He has supplied an additional reason for his prompt replacement. The Calles papers played up the benefits of his utterance in solidifying their government's security and promoting the inrush of tourists and other commercial gain; but the independent press harried him for his betrayal of American principles and his ignorance of Mexican facts.

After a month had passed and Calles had reaped the full benefit of his eulogies, Ambassador Daniels replied to the most upsetting of his critics, El Hombre Libre, August 20, that he had merely commended the extension of education, without any reference to its character, and he had cited Jefferson only to that effect. Surely the Ambassador who can not or will not see the evident effect, in all the glaring circumstances of his public commendation of Calles and his crew, and particularly regarding their most offensive and contested educational atrocities, is not fit to represent the United States nation, and our President should give a New Deal to the decent people of Mexico.

Before Mr. Daniels' significant eulogy of other
Mexican "patriots" receives due comment, an
equally timely boost of Calles and Company
from another important American source deserves mention. Ten thousand university students had assembled before the National Palace
in protest of the Government's usurpation of all
educational direction. Calling upon Calles and his
ministers in apposite but unquotable terms,
they denounced his "pederastic and sodomistic"
curriculum, and routed the police and soldiers he
sent to disperse them. Such manifestations, repeated elsewhere, were pregnant with peril; and
soon a New Yorker of important dual represent-
ativeness came to town, ostensibly on a vacation.

Calles Brings Booster from Gotham

Mr. Bernard Deutsch, President of the Board
of Aldermen and vice-mayor of America's great-
est city, and president of the Jewish Congress,
was feted in August by the Calles crowd, and in
turn he feted them, giving Mayor Aaron Saenz
place of honor over Ambassador Daniels, who
also graced the occasion. The New York Board
of Aldermen had passed a resolution, April, 1933,
against the "rampant persecution" of religion in
Mexico, asserting that "such action is uncivilized
and barbarous and unworthy of this age of enlightenment"; and in a public protest against
Hitler's treatment of German Jews Mr. Deutsch
had heard and sanctioned strong condemnation
of the worse Christian persecution in Mexico.
But after a four hours' session with Calles and a
trip involving a big business project, Mr. Deutsch
forgot all this, and proclaimed: "During my three

weeks' visit here I found no persecution of any class of people. Statements to the contrary are inexact."

Though 90 per cent of the churches before his eyes, and all Catholic schools and convents were confiscated and closed, and but twenty-five priests were allowed for the 1,700,000 Federal District population, and the functions of these were narrowly prescribed in church, and appearance in clerical dress abroad was a penal offense, Mr. Deutsch rang the changes to his banqueters on their Government's liberality and freedom, and he broadcasted to the world that, "Mexico's best advertisement was the stability of her democratic government, and the vigorous character of her industrial and commercial interests." Her gunmen rule and their statewide confiscations and robberies were "democratic government"; their drastic suppression of religion was not "persecution," because Calles told him so; and their commercial buiness was good because made good for Mr. Deutsch.

In fact the Jewish leaders vigorously denounced his statements and conduct. But he did Calles' work as effectively as Daniels in leaving the impression of American support; nor did he diminish the hostility of this ruling group, who, while they use Americans, hate them all the more.

This hostility is shared by Mexicans of the better class; and these have ample ground for it. A number of educated Mexicans of high standing, including an ex-governor who declined a presidential candidacy, told me that it was the consistent United States support of the bandit gang which accounted for their power and pre-

vented their overthrow; and they bitterly com-
plained of such ignorant supporting intrusions as
the Daniels-Deutsch incidents presented.

Our Ambassador's voluntary interposition in
favor of the educational program of Calles and
his puppet government would preclude Americans from thinking that the declared purpose
"to take possession of the consciences of the children and of youth" and thus "create a New National Soul" meant the clamping of his communistic dereligionizing teachings on every school in
the nation and prohibiting and stamping out all
others; and the projection of his eulogies on
American teachers made their intrusiveness more
indicative of United States sanction.

Mr. Daniels Further Manifests His Bias

He has made no apology. His explanation to
the Mexican editor was mere evasion, and his
reply to the State Department an irrelevant plati-
tude; yet Secretary Hull announced that the incident was closed. Should the citizens of the
United States who cherish the religious liberty
of their Constitution and the honor of their Government permit it to be closed, Ambassador
Daniels himself will not. He opened it more flagrantly and widely.

On October 19, 1934, both Houses of Calles'
Congress had not only approved the amendment
to their constitution socializing and de-religionizing the education of the land, but superadded
resolutions to expel all Catholic bishops and
clergy, confiscate all churches and institutions
not already plundered, and to consummate "the
creation of an Atheistic state by abolishing all

religion." Deputy Erro, whose proposal of these resolutions was adopted unanimously, thus introduced them:

"We must open the minds of the people by teaching them to see the world in the light of science. We cannot do this while the church makes them believe in God. We must tell them that God is a myth, a word, a grotesque thing."

To actualize this program, cut out opposition, and "take possession" of the minds and consciences not only of children and of youth but of all, he further proposed the suppression of the five independent journals that did not see eye to eye with "The Revolution." This resolution was adopted unanimously; and thus was freedom of religion and freedom of the press extinguished as effectively as congress and government could devise, and all other freedom was left shrieking more despairingly than in the Poland of Kosciusko.

Brings a U. S. Senator to Back Him

On that very day Ambassador Daniels walked into the Senate chamber escorting Senator Reynolds of North Carolina, and the Senate, by previous arrangement, interrupted its special session to receive the distinguished "Yanqui" Ambassador and Senator, as the Mexican journals designate them. A commission was appointed to escort them to the seat of honor, and the Senate President, Ortega, invited Senator Reynolds to address the assembly.

He did so effusively. "I deem myself highly honored," he said, "to meet such distinguished friends of a country that I have long admired and to deliver to them the greetings of the American Republic." In the presence of these, "the most illustrious representatives of this nation," he would state his conviction that, "this grand Republic is called to a great future and that complete success will crown the forces now directing its destiny." He foresaw United States visitors with their millions of dollars crowding into Mexico, at the same time enhancing its wealth and tightening the bonds of mutual friendship. It filled him with pride to address "the most renowned political leaders of Mexico" and he was overwhelmed with the privilege they had granted him.

Senator Padilla responded, expressing his appreciation of "the policy actually followed by the government of the United States and evidently intended to establish an understanding approachment between the Mexican Proletariat and the North American State"; and he commissioned Senator Reynolds to "present the cordial greetings of the Mexican Senate Chamber to the American Senate."

This preconcerted arrangement is eloquent of Ambassador Daniels' purpose to strengthen the impression he had previously created, that the American government and people stood behind the government of Mexico at the very time and moment it had by organic law or statute completely extinguished civil, social, religious, and educational liberty along with freedom of speech and freedom of the press.

All these iniquitous decrees and prohibitions were crowding the very papers that recorded Mr. Daniels' friendly visit to their perpetrators; and his subterfuge of hiding under the covering mantle of Senator Reynolds was clearly recognized by editors and people.

The extension of their prohibiting policy even to the freedom of the press might have given pause to an American who had long exercised as editor this guaranteed freedom of our Constitution; but for reasons seemingly occult, Mr. Daniels appears to have left American principles behind him and committed himself unreservedly to the full totality of Mexican tyranny.

It Is Question of Sanction or Recall

It would not matter if only Mr. Daniels' personality were involved, and his position had not made it appear that the American government authorized or approved his proceedings. With his repeated declarations in favor of the Calles program; with his refusal to withdraw a word of it despite the general outcry in the United States and the questioning from Washington; with the subterfuge through which, with Senator Reynolds, he put the blessing of the United States upon the Mexican Senate and government just at the moment that it had drastically consummated the destruction of all liberty; with all this glaring misrepresentation of our government and principles and people confronting them, how long will our President permit, how long will our people permit Josephus Daniels to align us with Calles and his gang and put the authority of our nation behind their communistic tyranny?

The further question arises, Why should we recognize a government subversive of all elemental rights by any ambassadorial representation?

Communism is no longer a visionary danger. The admission to the League of Nations of Soviet Russia, on which the Mexican system has been studiously modeled, has given to Communist practice as well as preachment, even in its extremes of atheistic tyranny, a world-standing and an impetus that the wisest thinkers of our time deem pregnant with disaster.

The recent American Legion convention has demanded by unanimous vote that our government's recognition of Soviet Russia be rescinded, on the ground that it provides dangerous facilities to her agents here to propagate their system at a time when unemployment and want are disposing millions toward any plausible panacea. These millions, thinks Mr. Woll, our most conservative labor leader, will rush into Communism should labor and sustenance be much longer denied them; and the fear is widespread that any notable failure of the New Deal would open or prelude the opening of Communistic floodgates. Then by what mysterious policy, one wonders, do we, while combating Communism within our doors, foster it in its worst form at our doorsteps?

The Communist Menace

That atheistic Communism permeates the government of Mexico was, as we have seen, the boast of Calles and his Congress; and that they are as intent as Russia in extending it beyond their borders is evidenced in a recent secret agreement by which Calles guaranteed to supply arms and forces to the expelled Vice-President of Nicaragua to usurp that government on condition of establishing there his own dereligionizing brand.

Our State Department can also gather from Mexican and Central American journals alarming reports of propaganda to like effect in the neighboring republics, and estimate how far Mexico's example and activities have reinforced Soviet propaganda in the United States.

These perils from our borders have been accumulating long and often by our own cognizance and countenance. Mr. Daniels could very well present in his defense a long line of American agents who gave like aid and comfort to the rabid governing minority in their one unifying purpose to uproot religion in Mexico; but his other statements and implications smacked more of the utterings of his Methodist friend, Bishop Cannon, than of historic truth. Mr. Daniels' laudations of Calles and of his conscience-killing system, just after that Supreme Chief announced its compulsory universalization by drastic organic law, was preceded by this paragraph:

"Mexico is today awake to the fact that its substantial future rests upon an educated constituency. Most of its troubles in past years, as is also true in other countries, can be traced to the failure of leaders of other days to educate its people. Whenever rulers have kept the mass of the population in ignorance, they have sown dragons' teeth and their countries reaped a crop of ills."

Mr. Daniels' Ignorance Prompts Further Insult

The falseness of his implication that the Catholic leaders of pre-revolutionary Mexico failed to educate their people is supplemented by Mr. Daniels' next sentence, in which he again ap-

plauds as truly Jeffersonian the Calles dogma:
"We must enter and take possession of the mind
of childhood, the mind of youth."

"Mind" is Mr. Daniels' milder version for Calles' "consciences," but its setting depicts his own
mind better than his reply to the Department of
State. It will probably be news to him that Calles
and his other friends "intrusted with leadership"
have, in their own drastic destruction of religion,
just completed the actuation of a plan of action inspired and in part drawn up by another United
States agent, also a Southern Methodist, over a
hundred years ago; and that it was precisely because free Christian education in school and college and university had, during three centuries
of religious and literary and artistic culture, per-
meated the mind and heart of Mexico, that our
first United States agent and Minister, Joel R.
Poinsett, plotted to destroy it for sinister political
purposes. It makes with its background and aftermath a lengthy story; but even in summary
form it will reveal the mainspring and the per-
manence of anti-Christian persecution by a tyrannous minority and provide the key to the modern perplexities of the Mexican problem.

The next chapter will present in outline the
astounding facts and feats of the Christian civ-
ilizers of Mexico.

CHAPTER III

THE CHRISTIAN CIVILIZERS OF MEXICO

WHEN Cortes entered Mexico three-fourths of its tribes lived in warring nomadic savagery, and the Aztec rulers offered yearly holocausts of from twenty to fifty thousand victims on their polytheistic altars. The transformation in a few decades of those mutually hostile nomads of many tribes and tongues into a settled Christian people, unified by the practices of a common faith and the arts and industries of a self-sustaining civilization, is one of the miracles of history.

The process is outlined in a pamphlet issued for the present writer by the International Truth Society of Brooklyn, **The Mexican Crisis, Its Causes and Consequences,** which traces the subversive aftermath to 1927. The historic entirety of the marvelous story may be found in **The Whole Truth About Mexico** and other works by Francisco Bulnes; in **Historia de Mejico** by Lucas Aleman, an historian and statesman, who was eye-witness to much of its development; in Carlos Pereyra's Histories of Spanish America, and in Father Cuevas' great **Historia de la Iglesia en Mexico.** It is also summarized in "Blood Drenched Altars" just issued by Bishop Kelley.

These authentic narratives will correct the

misrepresentations of many American writers,
who, unacquainted with original sources, have seldom permitted facts to modify their prejudices.

Missions and Schools Transform Natives

The apparition of our Lady of Guadalupe to a
lowly native, Juan Diego, on the outskirts of Mexico City, was undoubtedly the quickening stimulus to the rapid conversion of his fellow Indians;
but the advent in 1524 of fifteen Franciscans,
whom the natives styled "Motolinia" for the
poorness of their garb, followed by Jesuits, Ben-
edictines, Dominicans, Augustinians, with numerous sisterhoods, in establishing industrial
missions through the length and breadth of Mexico and combining secular with religious instruction in schools and colleges and universities,
mainly through the native tongues, will supply a
more natural if also supernatural explanation.

Typical of these missionaries and their activities was the Franciscan lay-brother Peter of
Ghent, kinsman of Charles V, who built numerous hospitals and asylums and industrial schools,
and had over a thousand natives in his great San
Francisco establishment in the capital. This de-
veloped into a college for higher studies, an academy of arts and crafts and a training school for
native teachers and officials, who went forth to
cooperate with the missionaries in bringing to the
tribes of Mexico, in their own tongue, the arts
and principles of Christian civilization.

Bishop Zumarraga's Santa Cruz College for
Indians, founded in 1534, which specialized in
Mexican languages, was but one of the many in-
stitutions that sent forth native mayors, gover-

nors, and teachers, to expedite the missionaries' progress. Bishop Zumarraga established in 1544, "since there are now so many who know how to read," the first printing press in the new world, whence he issued catechisms and school texts and the Bible in Indian, and numerous other translations and original works.

Arts and Crafts and First University

The University of Mexico, established in 1553, and leading Harvard by a century, required mastery of an Indian language for graduation, and produced, with its supporting institutions, a series of native poets, dramatists, historians, jurists, scientists and journalists, from the sixteenth to the eighteenth century, of an excellence that our contemporary North America had little to compare with. In the eighteenth century alone over seven thousand publications were issued, exclusive of three scientific and literary magazines; and a brochure by Dr. Castaneda of Texas University, on the comparative number and quality and output of schools and universities in prerevolutionary Mexico, and in our country at that period, supplies us many humbling revelations.

That industrial and agricultural development kept pace with religious and educational, is attested by the most exceptionally qualified and impartial witness, Baron Von Humboldt, the Prussian Protestant scientist, who issued in 1810 his **Political Essay on New Spain**, the result of his investigations and observations throughout Mexico. He notes that while one-fifth of the then several million population of the United States were Negro slaves, there were no slaves in Mexico, and its six millions contained but six

thousand Negroes. There are now but some fifty
thousand Negroes in a fifteen million population,
a significant effect of slavery's exclusion. It was
excluded by law and decree, again and again
repeated by Spanish Kings, and enforced by
heavy penalties; and though local abuses re-
curred when Spanish power was weakening,
Humboldt notes that these were exceptions to
the rule of free labor throughout Mexico.

Monuments of Mission Culture Everywhere

Humboldt found astonishing evidence of culture in the architecture that strewed the land.
His commentators note that the best specimens
exhibited to admiring visitors are confiscated
buildings of that period; and a ride over the
eighty mile drive from Mexico City to Puebla
will reveal every few miles a little church of
domed and steepled beauty, with often a hospital
or school or convent, built by the Indians whom
priest or friar had gathered around the hacienda
and transformed into settled and artistic workers.
The hacienda and its buildings are now held by
the Calles "acaparadores" (looters), and the natives have to steal in to pray in these monumental
witnesses to the faith and skill of their forbears.
Among the best exhibits in government museums
are paintings and statuary looted from these and
other churches.

Agriculture flourished with religion. Humboldt
pronounced the Indian farmer, who was "poor
but free," in a better condition than the peasants
of northern Europe, and deemed Mexico richer
in agriculture than in mines. The mine owners
and workers stimulated farm produce by enlarg-

ing the market and contributing to the erection
and maintenance of schools and hospitals and
works of beneficence. Aleman estimates the annual agricultural products at $30,000,000, and
Humboldt reports that, among other large ex-
ports in 1810, four competed successfully with
the United States. What a contrast to the Communist Mexico of 1934 that imports beans, eggs,
lard, corn, wheat, and fruit from the United
States!

Free Lands and Labor for Indians

In fact, it was pre-revolutionary Mexico that
was Communist or Communal, in the only sense
economically sound. Respecting the native Communal tribe system, Spain reserved from planting or building a circle of common lands sur-
rounding the villages; and beyond this Common,
called the Ejido, plots of thirteen acres were assigned to ploughmen for each yoke of oxen and
of five acres for workmen at their choice. Into
these assignments the missions gathered the nomads, protected by the Crown against grasping
Creoles. Official reports are frequent of the Mission Indians' prosperity as farmers and ranchers
and mechanics, assisted by the Pious Fund of the
Jesuits, until the Revolution grasped it with all
else, breaking the balance between Creole and
Indian; and Juarez in the fifties and Carranza
and Calles in our day seized the vast cultivated
acres for themselves and their friends, while the
less valuable lands thrown to the peasant workers (Obreros and Campesinos) were lost to cul-
tivation.

Our modern industrial reforms were also anticipated by centuries in Mexico. Phillip II ordained that a shift of eight hours be established by the sugar industry and of seven for mines; that the Indians have free bargaining, get a just wage, which must not be paid in merchandise beyond five pesos; that they must be maintained by employers during sickness; and that craftsmen must belong to a Guild or Union and their contract follow its rules (**Laws of the Indies, Book VI, Titles 10, 12, 15, Laws 16 and 19**). Thus was the best form of collective bargaining in force; and it was only under the revolution that the open shop began legally to operate. Humboldt sets the annual output, 1800-1810, in cotton goods, glass, copper, saddlery, etc., and of serge, baize, dyes and woolen fabrics, in which they competed with England, at thirty-five million pesos, and predicts a great future for the manufacturing centers. These then prosperous cities declined with the expulsion of the Spaniards, and land tenure changes and other grafting devices brought them further to present stagnation.

When Free Education Flourished

The laws that reduced the Indians to serfdom, extinguished education. The great University of Mexico (with which the present state institution has no connection), the solid scientific establishments and the Academy of Fine Arts, free to all races, which Humboldt pronounced equal to Europe's best, the great colleges and institutions and industrial Mission schools of Franciscans, Jesuits, Dominicans, Marists, Salesians, etc., for high and low of both sexes but mainly for the Indians, have been converted into barracks and tenements or wrested to the uses of the State or of its autocrats; and seldom has anything replaced them, except the crude Communist rural schools lately projected by Calles.

Though the vast institution of San Francisco in Mexico City, through which Brother Peter of Ghent, or de Gante, contributed most widely to Indian civilization, had covered many acres, you cannot find a trace of it now, nor even of the religious names of its buildings, except in Gante, one of the many streets that run through its site.

The same holds for the schools, hospitals and libraries, which the law required of monasteries and churches; for, says Prereyra, "to say monastery was to say school" (**Breve Historia de America**). The same law protected the Indians; and Decrees providing in minutest detail for their wage and care in farms, mines, factories, and towns, with privileges denied to the Spaniards, bestrew the **Laws of the Indies** under Charles V and his every successor for two centuries.

The Church, The Friend of Mexico

But though the maintenance of this vast system of mission schools, hospitals, etc., fell upon the Church, its income in 1810, as gathered from Humboldt, of $116,000,000 for six million people, compares favorably with the $272,000,000 income of the United States Baptists in 1916 for a like number of adherents. Humboldt mentions additional Church benefactions of irrigation works and aqueducts, and extols the hospital efficiency; but the hospital foundations in every town have gone with the expulsion of friar, priest, and sisterhood (cf. Cuevas, Vol IV). The fabled "rich-

es" of the Church, i.e., the institutions she rebuilt
after successive confiscations, are gathered more
thoroughly than ever into the present Communist
net.

Esquivel Obregon concludes his **"Influence of
Spain and the United States Over Mexico,"** with
an instructive tribute to Spanish beneficence in
the sixteenth century as exemplified in the superb
highway built from Mexico to Vera Cruz, in the
School of Mines erected by the mining guilds,
still an architectural jewel of the capital, and in
other contrasts between the productive country
of that day and the barrenness of the revolutionary period. "By their fruits, you shall know
them." Excelsior adds: "The erection of over
four thousand churches in two hundred and fifty
years, and hundreds of schools, convents, hospitals, and other beneficent foundations demon-
strates the supremacy of religion in the spirit of
the age. But, where are the roads, ports, irrigation works, political institutions and educational
systems comparable to those of colonial origin,
though these yield in grandeur and importance
to religion's architectural monuments?"

Religion's Work Sapped By Rulers' Greed

The rapid decline that followed the revolution
of 1810 was due primarily to the elimination by
a destructive minority of the religious influences
that had consolidated the barbarous tribes of
Mexico into one Christian and comparatively
civilized and prosperous people; and it is still
due to the same cause. To create hatred of the
Spaniards, grasping bandit leaders incited the
Indians by glorifying the civilization of their

Aztec ancestors, concealing the human sacrifice system and other Aztec barbarities; and the much over-rated Hidalgo, who led his ignorant followers to indiscriminate slaughter, somewhat atoned for his subversive and unpriestly career by this final declaration (Historia de Mexico, Aleman II, Appendix 32):

"I perceive the destruction I have wrought in the land, the dilapidation of the fortunes that have been destroyed, the enormous number of orphans I have left, the blood I have ruthlessly shed in such profusion; and my mind falters when I meditate on the multitude of souls doomed to the abyss for having followed me. I perceive that if you, deluded insurgents, persist in following the perverse maxims of the insurrection my punishment will be more severe, and the damage, not only to Mexico, but to yourselves as well, will have no end."

Religious influences had been declining since 1767, when the Jesuits were expelled by Charles III. Their long line of civilizing Missions was broken or abandoned, and their Pious Fund of some forty-five million dollars, which was lent to small farmers with its five per cent interest devoted to charitable and educational works, was confiscated to the State.

Iturbide, An Honest Unselfish Ruler

Though the consequent disorganization of education and agriculture and charitable works was deeply resented, yet, such was the general attachment to Spain that Mexico remained loyal to Ferdinand VII against Joseph Bonaparte, the

usurper of his throne; and it was not until the
Cadiz Constitution of 1820 restricted the rights
and liberties of the Church, and the liberalistic
Cortes rejected Mexico's submitted Guarantees
of Religion, Independence and Union, known as
the Plan of Iguala, that the Royalist leader Iturbide was proclaimed Emperor of an Independent
Mexico.

Iturbide was able and honest, and his unsel-
fishness is proved in his refusal of the immense
estates and other rich properties presented to
him. Events have absolutely verified his decision
that the people were not ready for American
Democracy and that absolute authority was requisite for efficient government in Mexico.

His one and ruinous mistake was in overes-
timating the importance of the turbulent minority, and, because he thought he had lost thereby
the confidence of the nation, in abdicating his
throne. He has been the only ruler of revolutionary Mexico who provided himself with none of
its wealth to solace his departure. It may be noted also, that the Mexican declarers of independence had grounded their claims on no such
"long train of abuses and usurpations" as Bri-
tain's Colonies had denounced, and far from
branding their king a tyrant, they sought continuance of Spanish rule under a prince of the royal
line, but without the foreign adventurers and
officials, nicknamed "Gachupines," against whom
alone lay the burden of their grievances.

First U. S. Envoy Plots Revolt

The organizer of the hostile turbulence that
prompted Iturbide to abdicate was Joel R. Poin-

sett, first American agent in Mexico, and first
United States Minister, 1825. He was the orig-
inator of a policy or system that has ever since
set and kept in power an unprincipled and tyrannous minority, and now that by law and government the Catholic Church is absolutely outlawed,
has just attained completely the consummation
he had set for it. His activities and their consequences demand the close attention of all American citizens who have the honor of their government at heart and would extend the principles of
its New Deal to our relations with our southern
neighbor, exercising true Americanism in its external as well as internal policies.

In an audience with the Emperor, Poinsett represented that Mexico should model itself upon
the United States in its form of government and
its political institutions; but Iturbide informed
him that the Mexican people, as was evident,
were quite different in their traditions and political capacities and that the United States system was altogether unsuitable for them. Indignant at this rejection of his wisdom and designs,
Poinsett characterized Iturbide, in his **Notes on
Mexico**, as a "most cruel and bloodthirsty persecutor of the patriots," and his government "'the
most glaring usurpation . . . not founded on
public opinion" (Cuevas, V, 132). It was from
these "Notes" that American writers formulated
the false tradition of Iturbide's ambitious and
tyrannous character.

Poinsett conceived "public opinion" as expressed by universal suffrage, which was utterly
impracticable in Mexico then, nor has yet been
put in practice; but back of this was a more sin-

ister conception. In 1812 the Spanish Minister in
Philadelphia, Louis de Onis, informed the Mexican Viceroy that the United States Government
had resolved to extend its limits to the Rio
Grande in the south and the Pacific Ocean on the
west, and the methods to be adopted for the execution of this plan are "seduction, intrigue, emissaries fomenting dissensions, instigating civil
war and furnishing arms and ammunitions to the
insurgents . . . Just now, the administration has
commissioned a talented lawyer of New Orleans
to cultivate relations with the insurgents in this
region" (Davalo, **Documentacion**, in Cuevas, V,
131).

Poinsett Yokes Masonry to His Annexing Plot

It is noteworthy that the boundary negotiations of 1848 coincide with these forecastings of
1810. The Onis memoirs further inform us that
the agent fomenting revolution in Mexico with
the object of uniting it with the American Federation was Joel R. Poinsett. Whether commissioned to promote revolution or not, it is certain
that Poinsett, when repulsed by Iturbide, incited
the leading factionists to procure his downfall,
insisting that freedom could be had only through
a federal constitution on the United States model,
in a land where neither states nor self-governing
colonies existed. To organize this hybrid government of greedy bandit leaders and divide the
country into states on a basis of reward for notorious revolutionists in the various localities,
Poinsett utilized a medium which has been working till this day with like effect.

This was the Masonic Craft. The Scottish Rite,
introduced by French officers into Spain, had

been brought to Mexico by some partisans of Ferdinand VII who plotted through this channel for the downfall of Iturbide. In Spain and in Mexico it was an occult political machine quite at variance with its social and fraternal character in England at that period, "and might be accurately defined a permanent conspiracy" (Historia, V, 5).

Noting its suitability for his purpose, but also the monarchical sympathies of its members, Poinsett secured authorization from the Grand Lodge of New York to install York Rite lodges in Mexico, and he initiated in these the men he deemed most adaptable to his designs. They emerged as the leaders of the "liberal," or religion-wrecking parties.

Though Henry Clay recalled and reprimanded him for these activities, Poinsett had left the party he organized drilled in the methods and assured of the effectiveness of a secret society as a political machine; and the National Masonic Rites, whether Escoses or Yorkino, played the principal role in Mexico's subsequent history. Thus, the public opinion that Poinsett pretended to foster became suppressed or thwarted by the plotting of sworn secrecy in the lodge, and the Masonry he had adroitly manipulated into a political machine for the "American Party" became, with the backing of United States Masonic Councils, the dominating influence in Mexican politics.

Would Destroy Church To Fortify Slavery

The then American Government was not responsible for Poinsett's politico-Masonic entanglements; and when rebuked for them by Henry Clay, he said he had been organizing patriotically an "American Party" (Cuevas, V, 136). It would seem he was rather forwarding the purposes of some Southern slave owners, who would annex Texas and Mexico's possessions not only above but considerably below the Rio Grande in order from these slaveless regions to form slave-holding states and thus fortify Southern slave-state dominance against the Abolitionist North.

Poinsett knew that people and clergy would not brook such a plan; hence the opposition must be weakened by division, and the powerful influence of the clergy must be eliminated. He had plotted the forcible usurpation of the presidency by Guerrero, the defeated candidate, and he instructed his government October 21, 1826, that Zavala, head of the Yorkino Masons and the pro-American faction, should be sent to control and direct the ignorant Guerrero.

Poinsett was convinced that for his purposes this direction should tend towards the undermining or extinction of the Catholic Church in Mexico. The faith of the vast majority, Spanish or Indian or mixed, was and is, very real in its patriotic as well as religious implications. Even the political journals today frequently recall the fact that it is through the Church they are the heirs of a great civilization and glorious past.

The domed and steepled temples that strew the land are a visible symbol of national unity and democratic brotherhood. Rich and poor, learned and illiterate, white and half-caste and Indian, can be seen kneeling shoulder to shoulder before its altars and reacting to the stimulus of the Christian civilization that hallows its holy places. The Mexican was seen to cling to his religion, as a buckler in defense of his traditions against the challenge of the materialistic giant of the North to crowd him from the land of his ancestors.

Masonry Allied To Extinguish Religion

Recognizing that religion was not a matter of superstition or sentiment for peons and gentry, but by conscience and instinct the central issue of the entire nation in its struggle for self-preservation, Poinsett and the pro-American liberal party he had organized adopted in secret session of the Grand Lodge La Luz in New Orleans, 1827, the following preamble and platform:

"Convinced that the clergy, inasmuch as it opposes colonization (of Texas by Americans), is a permanent obstacle to reform; that it impedes the diffusion of light, provokes antagonism toward foreigners (i.e., Joel R. Poinsett); . . . the Mexican National Rite adopts in all its parts the political plan and program of reform proposed by progressive men, which should be initiated in Congress as soon as possible by the Masons who hold seats there; . . . because, being based on the principles taught by Masonry, the Rite should redouble its efforts to make it effective in accordance with the terms in which it is conceived, namely:

"1. Absolute freedom of opinion and abrogation of all laws censoring the press.

"2. Abolition of special privilege for the clergy and the military.

"3. Suppression of monastic institutions and

all laws recognizing the intervention of the clergy
in civil business, such as the marriage contract,
etc.

"4.   Improvement of the moral condition of
the people by depriving the clergy of its monopoly on public education, by increasing educational
facilities and inculcating social duties by means
of the foundation of museums, art conservatories
and public libraries, by the establishment of educational institutions for classic literature, science
and morals."

Whose Freedom Is It?

Every one of these planks, carpentered by our
American agent over a century ago, is now in
the fulness of the sense intended a constitutional
enactment, and our present supreme representative honored the enactors by his presence on the
scene of their achievement at the moment of
completion. The first plank is legally concreted
in the absolute freedom of anti-Christian press
and speech, and the absolute suppression of all
other. Planks two, three, and four are realized
beyond even their expressed intent in the complete elimination of monks and monasteries and
Christian teachers and clergy, and the confiscation of all Christian churches, schools, and institutions.

The military are no longer banned since by
craft and graft they hold the motley army to their
clique, and the educational window-dressing is
supplied by the Calles "Conscience" curriculum;
but the true intent is now thoroughly enacted:
the complete uprooting by law and loot of Christian ministry and culture. How this consumma-

tion was effected in the intervening century is of vital interest today and will be reviewed in another chapter.

Meanwhile the vital question arises: While bishops and clergy and the best teachers and leaders and honest editors are being plundered, imprisoned, silenced, or cast penniless upon United States territory, does Mr. Daniels still maintain there is religious or other freedom in Mexico? And how long will the United States maintain him, and his policy and kind? These are no longer Catholic questions. The Living Church has voiced in living words America's duty to Mexico, and the long silence of our secular organs is broken. The El Paso World News, the Houston Chronicle, the New York Times, the Philadelphia Record, the Raleigh Times, the Christian Science Monitor, the St. Louis Globe Democrat, the American Hebrew, and numerous other journals have given space and thought to our Mexican problem, and the Literary Digest and Time have broadcasted the public findings. Policy as well as right demands an answer.

CHAPTER IV

How Our Support Put Persecutors In Power

VISITING Mexico some months ago, a correspondent of the **Houston Chronicle** was shocked to find its churches and Catholic schools and institutions confiscated, its clergy and religious and their teachings banned, an anti-religious education universally prescribed, and but a few priests permitted to minister, under severe restrictions, to what seemed to him a very religious and Catholic people. He noted the working of the ruling system against the will of a majority fervently religious; but none revealed to him the causes, least of all Mr. Daniels. The causative forces, which are the essence of the Mexican problem, start where the previous chapter left off, with the anti-religious program adopted in New Orleans at the Amphictyonic Council of La Luz and the Grand Lodge of Louisiana. Its direct relation to the present issue and to the United States policy that Poinsett formulated and Daniels has been actuating, will justify a somewhat lengthy disclosure of its workings.

Persecution Planned In Masonic Lodge

Among the signers or sealers of this oath-bound program to extirpate the Mexican Church in order to secure the domination of the Masonic pro-American party were Gomez Farias and Lorenzo Zavala, chief of the picked men whom Poinsett had schooled to his purpose.

When he was vice-president of Texas, Zavala sold a large portion of it for his personal profit to a New York land company, in the teeth of laws, enacted 1830, providing for colonization of Texas, but exclusively by Mexicans or foreigners of like traditions, and for fostering coasting trade therewith.

The promoter of these laws, against whom Farias and Zavala were marshalling all the resources of "Yorkino-Yanqui" intrigue, was Don Luca Aleman, the Conservative leader, who held that our governing system, however admirably adjusted to United States needs, was utterly unadaptable to Mexico. As the garment must be fitted to the man, not the man to the garment, so, he said, the organic laws of a nation must be shaped to its organism, not the organism to the laws. Hence a Constitution that is alien to the character, tradition, and genius of a people, will tend to the ruin rather than the peace and progress of that people.

Would Uproot Mexico's Catholic Culture

Farias and Zavala took the way of ruin. Eager to Americanize Mexico for their purposes, they would force its people into an unnatural and denaturing organic mould by eradicating the Catholic culture of three centuries, their one unifying bond, and thus fit them into a predetermined constitution of Masonic design woven into United States form from Amphictyonic stuff.

This attempt to remould, or rather de-Christian-
ize and re-paganize the Mexican people, has been
at the root of all Mexico's troubles and anarchic
conditions for a century; and it has never been
prosecuted so determinedly and ruthlessly as
now. This is Mexico's problem; and it will so
remain till the paganizing process is reversed
and constitution and government are readapted
to the nature and the wishes of her people. Poinsett's intrigues has foisted on States and Constitution American forms unnatural to Mexico,
and in 1833 the opportunity arrived to fill them
with Masonic content.

Forcing Lodges' Ban On Church and School

In the absence of Santana, the Conservative
President, executive power was assumed by
Gomez Farias, leader of the extreme left; and in
a month he had ordered the secularization of all
education in Mexico and closed the great university founded in 1553. The schools, which
covered the country so effectively that the prevalence of literacy astonished Humboldt, were all
sustained by the Church, and by long tradition
were Catholic to the core, and their teachers were
mainly religious; but Farias' decree stamped the
full force of his de-religionizing planks upon them
all. Farias followed this up by suppressing the
California Missions and confiscating the remains
of the Pious Fund and what else he could lay
hands on; thus opening the way to the ruin of
the Indians and to American annexation. He
completed his four-plank Masonic program by
decreeing that religious benefices must be filled
by civil appointment only and that all Bishops

and ecclesiastical heads must be nominees of the State.

Thus was first formally enforced, as far as decrees and laws could make it, the de-Christianizing plan, which Juarez was later to constitutionalize more clearly and Calles was to actualize to the furthest reaches of its atheizing logic. While providing well, like the latter, for his personal aggrandisement, Farias always grounded his autocratic perversions on love of the people and zeal for the public good, ringing grandiloquently the changes on liberty, equality, and brotherhood, and other catch-words of the kind his friend Poinsett had inculcated. Of this liberal stock-in-trade an opponent said with happy discernment: "When you hear fraternity, humanitarianism, philanthropy, reforming benevolence, etc., proclaimed, hide your children because Herod walks near by."

A New Herod In Mexico

They are hiding fearfully their children from the more murderous Herod that now stalks through Mexico to kill the consciences of their little ones; but stronger action was taken against Farias. The people rose in armed revolt in support of "Religion and Custom"; and though the "liberals" called it an organized effort of the clergy to obstruct reform, it was truly a popular reaction against the usurpation by civil government of religious jurisdiction. Defeated in the first attempt to enforce his four-point Masonic program, and deprived of his Vice-Presidency in 1834, Gomez Farias was summoned to New Orleans by Zavala, who was then promoting the secession of Texas and had a new plan for "the complete destruction of the ecclesiastical power."

On September 3, 1835, the Amphictyonic Council again held session at 103 Ursuline street, New Orleans. A Cuban filibusterer, called General Mejia, said the meeting was called in furtherance of their plan to recapture Mexico, replacing President Santana by Gomez Farias; and he informed them that the expedition was financed by various capitalists and landowners of Louisiana and neighboring states, on condition that Texas be transferred to these Southern States at a reasonable price, excepting the lands of Mr. Zavala and friends, with a view to ultimate annexation to "the new Republic of the South."

Farias feared that the plan of dismemberment would encounter overwhelming opposition from the national as well as clerical elements, but on the insistence of the others that the march on Tampico was already arranged and the monies were furnished, and the masses would follow whoever paid them best, their President designate signed his name to the compact. This, with the instructive report of the entire proceedings, may be found in the Farias collection of the University of Texas (Cuevas, V, 211-213).

The Church To Be Their Prey

The Council appointed Farias President of Mexico, and Mejia Commander-in-Chief "of all those who may be recruited in the State of Louisiana and on his way to Mexico," while Zavala was furnished arms and money to hold Texas in hand. It was ordered that Mejia, having captured Mexico, should keep his command under arms until the decrees which he should dictate to Congress be put in force. These decrees proclaim:

1. That the Constitution of 1824 be reformed in accordance with the Farias laws of 1833.

2. That all bishops and ecclesiastical or secular persons who are judged hostile to reform must leave the republic immediately.

3. That all cathedral chapters be suppressed, a governor of the diocese appointed, and silver and precious jewels delivered to the government.

4. That all convents of friars and nuns be secularized and suppressed, and their real estate and fixtures, silver and jewels shall be placed at the disposition of the government, and the buildings and chapels of the convents shall be utilized for asylums, hospitals, barracks, shops, or sold for synagogues and temples of other sects.

5. That all Mexicans be proclaimed free to worship God as they may elect, and all correspondence between the Government and Rome be suspended, but private individuals may continue as Catholics, providing they do not disturb public order or gain proselytes.

6. That two-thirds of all lands, rural and urban estates, be given to the indigent, preferably to the military, to whom will be assigned lands and houses sufficient to recompense their services.

7. There must be a close union and alliance with the United States of the North and their citizens, especially those of Louisiana, who will be held as brothers, admitted freely without necessity of passports, and refunded a third part of the import duties collected on the merchandise of other nations.

Typical Scheme To Ruin Church

This pact is trebly enlightening on all Mexican Revolutionary schemes: (1) It was not submitted to the people for ratification; (2) its primary purpose was to expatriate and extirpate the Church, despoil and confiscate its properties, and monopolize education for de-religionizing purposes; (3) it depended on United States aid to secure mastery of Mexico, and paid for it by treachery to its people.

We shall see that every subsequent revolution which succeeded secured that achievement by like means and for like purposes. Juarez was enabled to carry the plan a step further to enactment with an American army behind him, and Carranza with an American Army and Navy. Josephus Daniels is but a symbol of the forces that empowered or permitted Calles to stretch it to absolute totalitarian domination over press, person, property, and conscience.

Farias and his Cuban adventurer failed; but Zavala succeeded, with American aid, in wresting Texas from Mexico; and in 1836 he became its Vice-President. Thence to the annexation period, Conservative governments held Mexico in comparative peace while repairing much of the havoc wrought by "liberal" intrigue. Historians now agree with H. H. Bancroft that our war of 1846 was forced upon Mexico; but they know not or ignore the motivating causes, which are those indicated at the two Masonic Councils in New Orleans. The heroism at the Alamo and of brave Americans at other conflicts is deservedly remembered; but it is not even known that the refusal of Mexico to permit slavery in Texas was the main grievance of the heroes.

Mexican War To Consolidate Southern Slavery

Mexico had then, and ever, the "all free" status that Lincoln wanted for the United States; but the South wanted other territory that could be moulded into slave states. This, on the United States side, was the political cause for war and annexation; but these were incited and brought to focus by the intrigues of Poinsett and his disciples and the cooperating ambition of Farias to gain with United States aid the Presidency, and rule a de-religionized Mexico. It was their well grounded fear of this issue that united the conservative party against the invaders. It is well to observe that there was no "clerical" party at this or any other time, and that "conservative" included all who would conserve the religious as well as the other traditional observances of the people. This was summed in their battle-cry, Religion y Fueros, "Religion and Customs."

Santana secured the Presidency, with Farias Vice-President, and both might well be styled arcades ambo; but in this instance it was Santana that proved the patriot and Farias the traitor.

While Santana was rushing to meet Taylor with raw and unprovisioned troops, Farias was seizing the properties of churches, hospitals, schools, and all religious institutions, and mulcting the clergy by a $2,400,000.00 assessment. He sent but 37,400 pesos from his plunder to the hard-pressed Santana; and his purpose is made clear in his letter to the expelled Cabinet minister, Rejon, assuring him that soon their cause would triumph, for "Pegleg (Santana) with his cowardly army can do little against Taylor's strategy, bravery and intelligence. Taylor has the money; and he is in agreement with me, so you may count on the defeat of the Cripple" (Cuevas, V, 254; Archivo Farias, University of Texas).

Why Farias Fomented Dissension

It was to facilitate American entry that Farias was fomenting dissension and disorder; but when, on his expulsion, all other parties combined in earnest defense, churchmen melted down their gold and silver, contributing $2,500,000.00 to save their country from dismemberment. They proved themselves the truest patriots in the nation's need.

On the other hand, when the American Army entered the Capital, the Farias party seized the government, and Iriarte, their President, gave a banquet to General Scott and his staff, and, to the ill-concealed contempt of his guests, offered toasts to the success of American arms, the annexation of Mexico, and the destruction of the Church by United States assistance (Excelsior, August 9, 1926). They had already offered the dictatorship to General Scott; and the American Commissioner, M. P. Trist, reported them "resolved to play out their game of forcing our country into this (annexation)."

Farias left no stone unturned to fulfill thereby his New Orleans pact, and Senator Foster in Congress led a strong party in its favor; but anti-slavery agitation was against it, and President Polk was satisfied with retaining almost half of Mexico's original area.

Comparative peace followed the American treaty, and the Jesuit missions were re-established among the Chihuahua Indians; but the Farias party kept fomenting disorder in promotion of their plan, and they seized on the Gadsden Purchase of South Arizona as a pretext to rise in arms, though this Conservative transaction, however unwise, was quite in accordance with their own previous policy and pacts. Their leader, Alvarez, a licentious and brutal mulatto, ranks among the most repulsive and sanguinary characters in history, and his eulogy in Priestley's **Mexican Nation** disgraces even that historic travesty.

A "Human Panther" Starts Inhuman Tyranny

This fiendish "Human Panther," as he was termed, inaugurated his reign by the law "Juarez," abolishing ecclesiastical privileges; and he supported his successor Comonfort in expropriating under the law "Lerdo" all property and capital held in trust by the Church. The "Panther" further enabled the greedy Masonic minority to give this and its anti-religious conclusions a juridic entity in the Juarez code, which from 1859 to 1871 forms the basis and pillars of the constitutional edifice that Calles has but cemented and domed.

The Juarez laws abolished all religious orders and confraternities, dress, vows, teachers, and teaching, with practically all civil rights and legal personality; nullified Christian marriages, and penalized religious rites and insignia anywhere outside the Church walls. Churches and all religious institutions were declared the property of the State, which instituted a "National Church" of its own and invited United States sects to replace them; and "God" was eliminated from oaths and textbooks and civil formalities.

Under one of these edicts of 1859, the mayor of San Juan del Rio had several hundred pilgrims arrested in 1931 for reciting the Rosary in public, and in 1932 the Guadalajara authorities imposed a fine on laymen for appearing in the street on Ash Wednesday with a smudge of ashes on their brows.

But Church and State were not at all separated as Mr. Daniels implies. Constitutionally the State has swallowed the Church; it is but the physical swallowing that is now in operation. The public, to whom these laws had never been submitted, rose in violent reaction; and President Comonfort, who withdrew from the storm, confessed that "the constitution was enforced solely by coercion. . . The Nation repudiated the new Constitution and the troops simply sustained the Nation's will" (Cuevas, V. 315).

Buchanan Makes A Paid Traitor President

While the United States Commissioner, Forsyth, was negotiating for the cession of Lower California with the Comonfort-Juarez party and advising President Buchanan to support that party in Mexico "until such time as we are ready to Americanize her," the public reaction against the scheme brought the Conservatives to power.

The contemporaneous comment of the New York Times is instructive today:

"Before the fall of Comonfort various treaties had been negotiated with Mr. Forsyth, relative to a loan by the United States to Mexico, for the payment of which a mortgage was to be given on the State of Sonora, and arrangements made for a right of way over the Isthmus of Tehuantepec. If the liberal party returns to power * * * all those treaties can easily be put into effect * * * The United States may expect nothing in the way of treaties from the Church party, and Mr. Buchanan cannot fail to comprehend that it is good policy to support the liberal party."

This support, without which no "liberal" party ever gained or retained power in Mexico, was extended by President Buchanan to Benito Juarez, who had fled to Queretaro and there declared himself President. Driven from city to city, he fled the country. Nevertheless, when the Conservative Government refused to negotiate with the American minister for the purchase of several States, President Buchanan, deeming it good policy to support the complacent "Liberal" minority, broke off diplomatic relations with the established government and recognized the exiled Juarez as President of Mexico.

Juarez' Price For His Country's Sale

Juarez set out from New Orleans for Vera Cruz, where American recognition gave him his only claim to legality. He paid for it in signing the Protocol exacted by Mr. Buchanan's personal agent, W. M. Churchill, which guaranteed to the United States (1) the transfer of Lower California; (2) the right of way from El Paso to Guaymas and Mazatlan on the Gulf of Cali-

fornia; (3) alternate sections of land ten leagues
square on said lines of traffic, with military out-
posts thereon; (4) a perpetual right of way
across the Isthmus of Tehuantepec; (5) appor-
tioning a part of the monies received therefrom to
extinguishing Mexico's indebtedness to British
bondholders.

It was further stipulated that should either
government find its security endangered it must
summon the other to its support, and pay the
expenses involved; and each shall turn over dis-
turbers in their territory to the government af-
fected thereby. Under this provision a distinguished Cristero leader, who was tried and condemned in the United States for conspiracy
against the Mexican persecutors, was delivered
to Calles by the Hoover administration.

This McLane-Ocampo Treaty was, as Envoy
McLane makes clear in his reports, an intervention pact, under which President Buchanan aimed to replace the unamenable Conservatives by
Benito Juarez and his party, who would facilitate
the further formation of Slave States from Mexican territory (**Mexican Policy under Buchanan,**
Callahan 147-150; **American Historical Association Report, 1910**).

Buchanan Reinstates Juarez. Ensuing Outrages

The secession of South Carolina killed the
treaty, removing the Senators who would ratify
it; but this did not prevent Mr. Buchanan from
intervening decisively in favor of his protege,
Juarez. When the Mexican government had the
Juarez faction bottled up in Vera Cruz by sea
and land, the American fleet stationed nearby

attacked and captured the besieging Mexican ships, and having thus created the impression that the military forces of the United States stood behind Juarez, the plundering bandits everywhere flocked to his standard and restored him to power. The enormities committed by those bands of dregs and outlaws on a horrified people are unprintable, and their murders and mutilations of priests and their public rapings would fill columns. But Juarez wrote that though he regretted the excesses of his bandit partisans, they had served him well in destroying the resources of the enemy, and must be rewarded.

The usual confiscation and looting of Church and Conservative properties inured to the personal enrichment of the outlaws. In the federal district alone three hundred and ninety-seven urban and seventeen rural estates vested in teaching and benevolent institutions, were auctioned off to Juarez's picked partisans, who paid for them in worthless Government paper. This had become a routine celebration on "liberal" accessions to power; and the fact that they had forty-seven presidents in the thirty preceding years, 1829-1859, not counting rival chiefs of wider ravages, will give some conception of their ruinous devastations.

It was at this time that the most irrecoverable damage was inflicted on Mexico's school system, the oldest in all the Americas, and the best and most widespread for its period. Their successors had to pay for it, in part, when the Hague Tribunal in 1892 awarded a million and a half dollars compensation for their wresting of the Pious Fund Foundation from the California Missions.

But in Mexico the looting went on with the
wonted accompanying outrages; and Juarez applied his laws on the declared principle: "For
my friends, justice and favor; for my enemies,
justice only, if they can get it."

Protection Sought Against U. S. Interventions

Justice they could not get from Juarez's predatory party; and since their powerful northern
neighbor had directly intervened to put these
bandits in power and was arranging a pact of
perpetual intervention to sustain them, it is not
surprising that the Conservative body looked for
a balancing alliance that would enable them to
preserve their national integrity through a permanent stabilized Government that would rid
them forever of haphazard robber republics.

Juarez's attempt to replace the Catholic religion by a National Mexican Church, endowing
for that purpose its American Protestant organ-
izers with the great Church of San Francisco that
arose from the foundings of the venerated Pedro
de Gante, accentuated the general eagerness to
set effective barrier against the Juarez subverters
and perverters and their United States backers.
Finding the republican federal system unassim-
ilable in Mexico and recalling their prosperity
and cultural progress under a stable centralist
regime, the Conservatives determined to establish a dynasty strong enough to maintain order
within and to protect them against assailments
from without.

Good precedents were cited in England's choice
of the German Hanover, Sweden's of the French
Marshal Bernadotte, and Belgium's of Leopold

of Saxe-Coburg; but Mexico's foreign selection proved less fortunate. At first Archduke Maximilian of Austria was received with acclaim by the people, especially by the Indians, who saw in him a savior and restorer of their religious and racial inheritance. But their chosen Catholic champion was found to be a Mason; and his maintenance of the Juarez code in violation of the pact to restore the ancient laws and rights of Church and people, and his retention of the pro-liberal Council and a foreign army under Bazaine and other Masons soon lost him the support of the Conservatives, and would have insured his fall without United States interposition.

U. S. Armies Again Impose Juarez On Mexico

The obvious intention of Napoleon III and of England to weaken or divide the United States by this arrangement, as the Buchanan slave dynasty had tried to divide and weaken Mexico, rendered hostile the Republican government which had just abolished that dynasty; and Juarez, while cultivating Masonic friendship with the imperial court, was fomenting disturbances to provide pretext for American entry (Bulnes; El Verdadero Juarez, 864).

Lincoln and Seward refused at first to supply him arms or money, telling his envoy that "every million the United States should furnish would cost Mexico the loss of a State, and every rifle an acre of mine lands." But when Marshal Bazaine, the Masonic friend of the "liberals," withdrew his French army, and the Conservatives under Miramon and Marquez had put Juarez to flight and assumed effective control, General Sheridan was sent with a powerful army to the Rio Grande in support of Juarez and his fleeing partisans.

Sheridan tells us in his **Personal Memoirs** that he strewed military stores for the refugee chiefs along the border and that "the support given to their cause in this form encouraged them to renew resistance when all hope had disappeared" (II, 216-228). It was thus we reinstated a rabid minority in a miscalled "Republic," the antithesis of ours, and forcibly ousted the National Government whose principles were essentially our own.

United States Propped Juarez Tyrannies

We so continued, despite the assassination of Maximilian and of the Conservative leaders, whose only consolation was what Miramon wrote to his wife: "My beloved, I have received God's Body and am filled with confidence in His Mercy."

Our favor held through the ensuing decade while Juarez and his understudies were raping institutions and property and murdering their foes under the "Ley Fuga" they had invented, and, through their Juarez code, were extinguishing all the religious liberties and Christian ministry and teaching that law and force could reach.

The accession of Porfirio Diaz in 1876 interrupted priest-baiting and Church robbery. The Juarez laws remained; but Diaz so tempered their incidence that the Church could function quietly and lead an underground life unmolested. Reconstructing anew from a dozen confiscations, she was conducting at the end of the Diaz period some 2,000 free schools and colleges, practically all the rural schools, and a new network of hospitals and institutions maintained free by clergy and sisterhoods dependent entirely upon charity.

We shall see how all these free institutions of enlightenment and beneficence were swept away and despoiled by the robber bands whom our armies and navies and munitions and multiple support put and kept in power.

CHAPTER V

How Mr. Wilson Let Guarantee of Liberty be Scrapped

THE peace and prosperity which Diaz established enhanced in the eyes of the Church his constructive toleration; but his favor towards foreign enterprise begot the jealousy of greedy natives and disappointed American exploiters. Hence, in 1910, when the riches of Mexican oil fields were realized, hostile factions, backed by our Masonic and other elements intolerant of his tolerance, filled the American press with the infamies of Diaz absolutism, and with American arms opened the Madero-Magon revolution on our borders. Had our United States Government exercised then half the energy it displayed in arresting the border movements against Obregon and Calles, the Madero-Magon operations could not have started.

But Madero disappointed his promoters. He really wanted a free democracy by honest elections; and as these seemed certain to put the Catholic Union in control, a new revolution started on our border, again with American arms and munitions.

The Washington administration was said to have become unfriendly to Madero on the same ground that had made it grow hostile to Diaz. The latter had refused, and the former had failed in his promise, to ratify the lease to the United States of Magdalena Bay in Lower California. Disappointed political and concessionaire exploiters had also their influence. Again we sacrificed to our material interests the civil and religious rights of the Mexican people.

President Wilson Hounds Down Huerta

The scheme failed for the moment, when an attempted revolution by a nephew of Diaz resulted in the presidency of Huerta, who by his firmness and justice so satisfied the orderly elements that he was recognized by England and Germany and the majority of stabilized governments; and United States recognition, urged by our Ambassador and consuls, awaited only the inauguration of a new executive. Instead, President Wilson supported with army and navy the worst scoundrels that ever raped and pillaged Mexico; whence issued the orgy of anarchy and tyranny that culminated in Calles.

Victoriano Huerta had his faults; but it was not these that moved Woodrow Wilson to destroy him. A commission of Mexican and United States Masons, headed by Governor Reynoso of Guanajuato, called on President Huerta to assure him that if he rejoined the Masonic body and accepted their platform they would secure him United States recognition. Taking a scapular from his breast, Huerta said, "No; I am a Catholic, if a poor one, and that is my platform." His opening of Congress, for the first time in the name of God, and his urging its members to pray and legislate so that God's law should reign, further hardened Masonic hostility.

Having crushed decisively the rebellions which these agencies and President Wilson's antagonism had excited, President Huerta proceeded to govern with such even-handed efficiency that

Ambassadors Wilson and O'Shaughnessy reported a new era of peace and stability. They added that triumph for Villa and Carranza could only issue in anarchy; yet, while these and their ruffiandom were everywhere desecrating, murdering, and plundering, holding and torturing priests for ransom or death, and raping even cloisters, President Wilson raised the arms embargo in their favor.

U. S. Forces Make and Break A President

This, with a stringent and watchful embargo on their opponents, had been the usual American method of putting and keeping Mexican "liberals" in power; but it failed to make headway for Carranza. Then President Wilson launched an action which makes his name and administration hateful to decent Mexicans today and reft of hope the patriotic majority, who, at every crisis, feel the giant hand of the United States withholding them from recovering their country. Through his then Secretary of the Navy, Josephus Daniels, he sent the United States Navy April 21, 1914, to seize Vera Cruz and later Tampico, Huerta's only channels for supplies; and so, by armed intervention, Carranza and spoilsmen were hoisted into power.

The pretext that Huerta murdered Madero seems as groundless as his constructive insult to our flag; and execution of a predecessor did not preclude recognition from Carranza and Calles and many others to whom we had no scruple in extending it. But Lane Wilson shows in "Diplomatic Episodes" that Madero was spirited away and slain by friends of Generals Ruiz and Reyes in revenge for his or his brother's execution of these and other officers; and the actual assassin, Cardenas, was made a Brigadier by Carranza. The New York World had "scooped" the specific details for publication; but it was compelled to suppress them by order of President Wilson, who exercised a closure on the American press regarding Mexico that continued to our day and is but now beginning to be broken.

How Wilson Constitutionalized Gangsterism

It was said that their libertarian slogans appealed to him. They were the "Constitutional" party; for like their Calles continuators they were fluent in fine labels that belie the contents. Their gangsterism is labelled liberalism; their agrarian brigandage is peon emancipation; their state swindling is national finance; their Communism is concentrated Capitalism; their free education is compulsory de-Christianization; and their freedom of thought is atheism gone totalitarian. Carranza's "Constitutional" label was accepted by Mr. Wilson as genuine, despite his replies to Cardinal Gibbons admitting the extent and enormity of that party's crimes against life, liberty, and religion. These were but regrettable incidents in the great cause of constitutionalizing Mexico by putting the Constitutional President out and forcing the most unconstitutional in.

So set was Mr. Wilson on this, that, according to Colonel House, he forced Congress to reverse its position on the Panama tolls by imposing the same tolls on American shipping, so that England in return should withdraw her recognition of Huerta and thus facilitate, as Mr. Bryan put it, "the elimination of Huerta by one process or another." This done, the murderous Carranza, though he rejected the Wilson conditions, was installed; and he was duly recognized even after he had perpetrated the 1917 Constitution, an instrument more destructive of religious liberty and all human rights than the Penal Laws that Burke found exhausting "the perverted ingenuity of man."

Daniels Renews Anti-Wilson Memories

Our recognition and support of Carranza's successor and of other murderers will be treated in another chapter; but the present situation makes notice of one feature in our anti-Huerta campaign apposite here. President Wilson's Secretary of the Navy, who sent our warships to Vera Cruz and directed our marines against Mexico's President, was Honorable Josephus Daniels. This unfortunate selection was felt to be a reminder to the anti-Calles majority of their previous humiliation, and a pledge to the Calles regime of our unfaltering support.

Mr. Daniels has justified their misgivings and verified their fears. He has been reviving by word and act their sorest memories. His spontaneous eulogy of Calles and his puppets and their policies and practices has renewed the bitterness of Wilsonian animus; while his silence on their final extirpation of all liberties and spoliation or expulsion of clergy and opposing laity, seems eloquent of United States approval.

Hence the impatient questions that have been multiplying from press and platform concerning him. Hence also the urgent duty of our citizens, the ultimate sovereigns, to continue their insistence by demand and protest that their Government servants shall restore in Mexico the honor of our country.

Our Share In Constitutional Monstrosities

It has been shown by documented proof that our first United States Envoy organized a Masonic political machine for dominance of Mexico by ousting the Catholic Church and its culture from school and temple and the hearts of its people, and by securing therefor the armed forces of the United States at the price of half its territory and of preponderance over all.

We have also seen how the price was paid, and how from Buchanan to Wilson we furnished arms and armies and whatever other aid was requisite to empower bandit factions to eradicate religion and culture and civil liberties.

Mr. Wilson differed from his predecessors in making his intrusions work directly to this effect by empowering and sanctioning the Carranza Constitution of 1917. Mr. Yon Lind had wired him to bring the rule of intellectuals to an end. His own confidential agent to Carranza, a Methodist preacher named Silliman, wrote in like tone; and The United States Foreign Relation Papers of 1914, sq., which make humiliating reading, show their principals eagerly following these agents' advices; but Duval West of San Antonio, their only agent that told them the truth, was recalled.

There were no intellectuals at what they called the Constitutional Convention of Queretaro, but there were ex-lawyers, who, like the other members, had won representative right by pillaging distinctions, and were keen to concoct a legal contrivance that would guarantee their plunder and perpetuate the plundering. This they did in the 1917 "Constitution," an extension into organic law of the worst enactments in the Juarez Code against religion and liberty.

Though devoid of every constitutional character, having been imposed by self-nominated bandit chiefs who pistoled the few moderates into silence and never submitted it for ratification, this monstrous instrument has living interest today both as the basis for Calles' organic and executive monstrosities, and as a Wilsonian legacy which no successor of Mr. Wilson has yet disowned and which the Secretary of his then empowering Navy is now sedulously guarding. How sedulously Mr. Daniels is caring in our name for the child of his fostering will appear when we have made some study of this constitutional monster whose potencies Calles has actualized and applied systematically in totalitarian destructiveness.

The Juarez Code Tyrannies Extended

The Juarez Code, though intentionally prohibitive of all religious rights, left loopholes here and there through which churchmen and others marked for despoilment might enter claims for possession or indemnity, and it failed to afford sufficient scope to the war chiefs of the Villa pattern for legalized plunder. This the Carranza Constitution fully achieved; even though Carranza himself was more the tool than the chieftain of the plunderers. Picked by the bandit chiefs whom our navy and army and monies and diplomacies had lifted into power, the members of the convention represented but the motley forces we had armed and paid for, and certainly not a half million of the fifteen million population.

This crude misrepresentation achieved, however, one result of permanent and perilous importance. Dropping the smoke screen of "Constitutionalist," which had been thrown up to accommodate Mr. Wilson, they called themselves the National Revolutionary Party; and, claiming to represent all the people of Mexico, they initiated the Calles dogma that the P. N. R. (Partido Nacional Revolucionario) was the one and only party permissible, and there cannot and must not be another.

Calles interprets "Nacional" to mean that all Mexicans are born into his Revolutionary Party, and, by Constitutional birth-bond, their "Consciences" also "belong to the Revolution." They thus founded a one-party dictatorship as exclusive as the Nazis in Germany and the Communists in Russia, with the same totalitarian trend. Hence, any opposition to their laws or methods of executing them or to the organization itself, is termed treason and is penalized as such. It was on these premises that the recent protest of Archbishop Ruiz, the Apostolic Delegate, against the atheizing educational amendment and other dereligionizing acts and decrees, was met by an order for his arrest and imprisonment. A sentence to death, which governors and deputies have been urging for all prelates and priests, would be an equally logical penalty.

Sheeps' Wool Thin in Wolfish Constitution

The first article of the 1917 Constitution, which still stands, restricts the right of every individual to "the guarantees which this constitution grants," thus setting itself against the fundamental principle of the United States and of all other democratic governments, that civic and natural rights are inherent in the individual and that sovereignty reposes in the people and not in the constitution, which merely declares it. Mexico's Constitution is thus a party document which grants to the people only what the party decrees. The third article, forbidding all but laic education, has been supplemented by the Calles amendment of 1935 "to exclude all religious doctrine and combat fanaticism and prejudices," that is, all religious practices and beliefs.

This expresses better the mind of the Queretaro Deputies; but their immediate purpose was obtained by legalizing the robberies of the chiefs and their subordinates. The lands and properties they had "occupied" were declared "expropriations for public utility"; and their extension of this principle to the future through the right to limit private property by "public interest norms," with no prescribed indemnification, made government robbery unlimited, and left an open road to whatever communism it should select.

Flouting of Recognition Conditions Overlooked

President Wilson informed Carranza that American recognition would be conditioned on the fairness of the constitution's provisions for foreign rights and financial obligations, for amnesty to opponents, and for "the Roman Catholic

Church" and "priests or ministers of any church, and that only "just land tenure, free schools, and true freedom of conscience and worship" will "command the moral support of America". The effort which Carranza made to have these principles enacted, cost him his life; and despite their replacement by an instrument that constitutionalized persecution and robbery and obliterated the rights of the vast majority to liberty, property, and life, that constitution, with the presidents that championed it, received full United States recognition as it does now in its still more tyrannous form.

The labor clauses of the 1917 constitution, which read like extracts from Pope Leo's Encyclical on Labor, look astonishingly well in print; but they have proved in practice to have little other merit. In the hands of autocratic grafters they have been utilized, on the one hand, to catch the mob by glowing promises impossible of fulfilment, and, on the other, as a political club to wrest property and graft from employers and proprietors, and employes. Obregon gloried in the boast, "my division has crossed the Republic between the maledictions of friars and of the middle class." The 1917 constitution provided him and his kind with further glory.

We have seen that Deputy Erro grounded the "education" amendment on his party's dogma that God and religion were myths and grotesque superstitions that must be "defanaticized." He was but repeating the professions of the Queretaro deputies, who denounced all religion as a corrupting farce and confession as adultery, and sang such ribald distichs as, "if ropes we lack for tyrants' necks, we'll plait them out of friars' guts." It was in this spirit that provisions against property and priesthood were enacted.

The clauses in Article 27, which decree retro-actively that direct domain of all mineral lands belong to the nation and ownership therein to Mexicans only, moved Ambassador Sheffield to insist that the lands and rights of Americans must be respected.

Silent On Guarantee of Religious Rights

It was in reference to this clause, which was troublesome to American oil magnates and other concessionaires, that Secretary Kellogg stated in 1925 that the government of Mexico was on trial before the world; but its immeasurably worse and more indefensible spoliation of church and clergy and religious properties excited him to no such utterance. His silence was the more sinister, that he had before him the required guarantee for recognition of the Carranza gov-ernment given to Secretary Lansing, October 8, 1915, that they "will respect everybody's life, property and **religious beliefs**". On the religious beliefs guarantee, our government is still silent.

The same article deprives religious associa-tions of all right to have or acquire real estate, and nullifies all legal acquisitions by churches or members of religious cults since 1856; and con-tracts of all kinds from 1876 are made revisable, thus leaving an open field for universal graft. Of this, Obregon and Calles became the most not-able beneficiaries.

Article 24 proclaims that all men are free to profess the religious belief they prefer and to practice it in temple or home; but every religious act of public cult must be performed within the temples only and always under the vigilance of the authorities. They send out the first part of this for foreign consumption; but whatever value the restrictions of the second part leaves in it is completely eliminated by article 130.

Church Shorn of All Rights

Premising that the federal power has the right to exercise in all matters of religious cult whatever the law prescribes, it establishes sixteen proscribing laws, which are, in summary:

Marriage is merely a civil contract pertaining to the civil authorities exclusively. "The law recognizes no personality whatsoever in the religious groups denominated churches"; and "ministers of cults will be considered as individuals exercising a profession and will be directly subject to whatever laws may be promulgated therefor." State legislatures will determine the maximum number of ministers of cults; and only a Mexican by birth can officiate in Mexico.

Ministers of cults may never in public or private meeting, or in acts of cult or religious propaganda, criticize fundamental laws of the country, the authorities in particular, or the government in general; nor may they exercise active or passive vote or the right to associate for political ends.

No place can be open for public cult without permission from the Department of the Interior, and no change of minister in any temple can be made without Government sanction, under penalty of dismissal and fine of 1,000 pesos for each infraction by the municipal authority. Under no conditions will studies in seminaries of cults be recognized or sanctioned or revalidated.

No publication of a religious character may comment upon national political affairs or the acts of the country's authorities and administrators; and "the organization of any kind of political party whose title may contain a word indicating some relation to religion is strictly prohibited."

"No minister may inherit directly or through third parties, or receive by any title, a building occupied by associations for religious or beneficent purposes; and all ministers of cults are legally incapacitated to become heirs of other ministers or of any private individual not related within the fourth degree. The movable and immovable property of clergymen and religious associations is subject to acquisition by private individuals under article 27 of the same constitution."

Making Proscription of Liberty Air-tight

One would think perverted ingenuity could extend no further its proscriptions of the Church in person, property and function; but Carranza's "Constitution" found a way of delegalizing whatever rights might remain, by this final clause: "Any process for the infraction of the foregoing statutes is not subject to trial by jury."

In other words the Catholic Church has no legal redress, and organic law puts its sisters, teachers, and institutions and entire activities, outside the pale of law. All these proscriptions still hold, hardened and enforced by Calles' airtight specifications and penalties.

On the ground that "the majority of the people, the better classes and the bulk of the middle classes are still against the Revolution," Deputy Narvaez proposed to abolish trial by jury for journalists also, as it would mean immunity for the enemy press and they had the power to protect their own. This argument secured deletion of trial by jury from Article 7 and its retention in 20 only as a "privilege."

The correctness of the Deputy estimate that the majority were against them may be gathered form the fact that one still hears constitucionalista commonly pronounced con-su-uña-lista, that is, "with your claws ready to grab." It is also instructive that the word "to graft" became Carranziar in Mexican vernacular; and the Calles activities have but intensified this connotation.

The Carranza Constitution's expropriation to the State of all churches and religious institutions applied to edifices and properties so recognized and titled. The Calles party, by practice for a decade and now by constitutional amendment, have extended it to all private residences where Mass has at any time been offered or any form of religious instruction given, with the result that when church seizures are exhausted, his spies and grafting agencies have still an open field. Cardenas has further enlarged their facilities by decreeing state reward to the spies and confiscation of all properties wherein they report religious service has been held or priests have been sheltered.

CHAPTER VI

MASONIC BACKING OF CALLES' SCHEDULE

ARTICLE 3 of the 1917 Mexican Constitution is the main avenue that Calles has seized for the permanent uprooting of religion from the minds and hearts of Mexico. This article abrogates the parents' right to provide for the education of their offspring; and on this quite justifying basis, Calles proclaimed, and by organic law has since executed, his purpose, "to enter into and take possession of the consciences of the children, of the consciences of youth," and "to create a new national soul," and compel all Mexico "to belong to the revolution."

Thus, also, was finally realized in its fullness the plan of action set by Joel R. Poinsett and adopted in 1827 by the joint Mexican and American Supreme Masonic Councils in New Orleans, namely, to abolish the privileges of the clergy and all laws recognizing intervention of the clergy, and "to deprive the clergy of its monopoly on public education."

This meant, as the context obviously shows, that the Church must be kept out of the schools, and religion out of all education, so that the State shall mould the pupils to its will. This was precisely the purpose of the Farias decrees of 1833, of the Juarez code of 1857, of the Queretaro Constitution of 1917, as of the Calles amendments of 1934 and of the high Masonic Councils before and after 1827. And all were based on the same ground, that the child belongs not to the parent but to the State, and that the State alone has the right to educate him, the parent not at all.

Masonic Doctrine That State Owns Child

Calles has set the meaning in franker wording, that "the child belongs to the revolution," that is, to his own National Revolutionary Party, and he has provided thereby to force the whole State into his party and so create a "new national soul," atheistically totalitarian.

That the child belongs to the State, and that the State has the sole right to educate him, and that all religion must be excluded from his teaching, is a primary Masonic doctrine, not only in Mexico and Latin countries, but here. In Spain and France and other Latin lands the first sign of Masonic dominance is the exclusion of the crucifix from the school and the replacement of Christian by anti-Christian teachings. United States Scottish Rite Masonry has been always in union with the Grand Orient and in sympathy with this policy, and all American Masonry is in formal union with it now. It will, however, be news to the vast majority of United States Masons that they are officially committed to the same principle and to its practical adoption in our schools, despite a decision to the contrary by the Supreme Court of the United States.

The Supreme Council of the Thirty-third Degree in Washington and the Imperial Council of Oregon, having resolved in 1920 that education in religionless public schools must be made compulsory on all, both started an agitation for a law in Oregon compelling public school attendance for all children from 8 to 16. They assumed the credit for its adoption in 1922 and had similar bills ready for other States. They were legally represented at the injunction proceedings in Oregon and at the appeal therefrom to the Supreme Court of the United States.

Supreme Court Sustains The Parent Right

The court of last appeal also declared the law unconstitutional, and Justice McReynolds thus voiced their unanimous opinion June 1, 1934:

"The fundamental theory of liberty upon which all governments in this union repose excludes any general power of the State to standardize its children by forcing them to accept instruction from public teachers only. The child is not the mere creature of the State; those who nurture him and direct his destiny have the right, coupled with the high duty, to recognize and prepare him for additional obligations."

The unmistakable affirmation by the United States Supreme Court that this specific parental right is inalienable by constitution as by nature, was acclaimed throughout the nation as the final seal on a priceless American principle. But not so the Scottish Rite, whose Supreme Council presents a more binding allegiance to its brotherhood than the Supreme Court or Constitution of the United States.

In "American Masonry and Catholic Education" (International Catholic Truth Society, Brooklyn, N. Y.), this writer has shown the constant aim of United States Masonic chiefs to establish compulsory state education on the basis of the State's predominance over family and individual rights, though quite aware of its double discordance with the Constitution.

Supreme Masonic Council Defies Supreme Court

No sooner had the Supreme Court ruled out this Masonic doctrine as the direct antithesis of our "fundamental theory of liberty" than the Supreme Council of the Thirty-third Degree issued in Washington a counter pronouncement in defiance of the Supreme Court of the nation. Ignoring the court's characterization of their own educational ends and principles as destructive of our natural and constitutional rights, and harping irrelevantly on educational needs, this Masonic Council of American citizens rejected categorically the Supreme Court decision, and issued a profession of principles and purposes which Calles and his Mexican Masons could not better:

"We are, therefore, justified in continuing to assert and maintain our belief in the value of the compulsory requirement of attendance of all children upon the public schools. * * * We cannot at this time but insist upon the existence of the principle that the right of the child to avail himself of the educational opportunities of the public school is superior to the right of the parent or of any corporation, secular or religion, to shape in advance his intellectual allegiance and we should be alert to unite with every movement which tends to the maintenance of this right."

They have been so alert. The masters of American Masonry have supported every movement in

France and Portugal and Spain, and especially in
Mexico, to force irreligious and anti-religious
education on the child, and their 33rd-degree organ, **The New Age,** is a vigorous backer of
Calles' compulsory educational communism. It
issues a monthly bulletin proclaiming their cardinal purpose to bring about the compulsory
education of all United States children in religionless schools controlled and supported by a
centralizing federal department.

This, clearly, is to Mexicanize American education on Calles' communistic plan. Hence the
timeliness of the recent pronouncement of the
American Hierarchy:

"We cannot but deplore the expressions unwit-
tingly offered, at times, of sympathy with and
support of governments and policies which are
absolutely at variance with our own American
principles. They give color to the boast of the
supporters of tyrannical policies, that the influence of our American government is favorable
to such policies. We do not believe, for a moment, that it is. It could not be. * * * No upholder
of the rights of man can view complacently the
exercise of such tyranny, even though it be in a
country other than our own."

Sinister Workings of Supreme Masonic Council

But the Supreme Council of the Thirty-third
Degree is no upholder of the rights of the Catholic or Christian man. Controlling officially three-
fourths of the United States Masonic territory,
and virtually all of it through the representative
center at Washington, its strategic position en-
ables the Supreme Council, however unwarrant-

ed, to pose as the authorized mouthpiece of the three million voters who are Masons, and thus, through a wide variety of channels and approaches, to exercise an occult but potent influence on legislation and policies and administrative appointments. It has exercised that influence consistently in favor of Mexico's anti-religious factions; especially in behalf of Calles, whom it has elected to its Thirty-third Degree, and honored with the medal of highest Masonic distinction.

It is time that our citizens take action on the underground activities of these oath-bound potentates who proclaim their set purpose to uproot our basic constitutional principles; and such action devolves primarily on American Masons, who, in the vast majority, are Americans first, and have never authorized nor would knowingly suffer any Supreme Council to tamper with their loyalties.

It was after the Supreme Council's deputies had assured Carranza of United States support and their Supreme Grand Master had pledged the services of World Masonry for the Bryan-Wilson arbitral peace plans, that President Wilson said he could not "sympathize with those who attempt to seize the reins of government for the benefit of their selfish interests and ambitions." Yet this is precisely what he effected, actualizing his sympathies by overwhelming force, and making the 85 percent or more whom he professed to champion the victims of ambitious bandit chiefs who could muster and munition robber armies through his aid.

Pledge-Breaking Assassins Recognized

Their subsequent procedure closely corresponds with Mr. Wilson's own description of the Southern Carpet Bagger regime in his History of the American People, Volume V. The difference is that "the postbellum nightmare" endured but a decade; but Mr. Wilson's coercive intervention in Mexico's internal affairs resulted in making the worse nightmare he thereby inflicted perpetual. Whether by the influence of high Masonic Councils who knew how to utilize their uninformed three million membership, or of fanatic bigots in their heyday of political power, or of oil speculators and bankers and other grafting concessionaires, the heirs of Mr. Wilson and Secretary Bryan have prolonged and intensified the nightmare, and Ambassador Daniels has pronounced it a happy condition of national activity.

It was only when Carranza, who shared with the other Revolutionists we have thrust into power a bitter hatred of the "Yanquis", attempted as President-unelect to moderate the persecuting clauses of his Constitution, that he lost American support. Though Carranza was recognized on condition of establishing justice and liberty, we soon gave full recognition to the successors who had murdered him and extended and hardened the persecuting clauses of his Constitution.

The then Bishop Diaz thus admirably characterized that instrument: "In synthesis, the present Mexican Constitution is simply the unchecked expression of a savage political theory, implanted by an egotistic oligarchy, to give color of legality to their malignant actions."

Admitting that it extinguished "liberty of conscience and inalienable human rights," Carranza urged his Congress, December, 1918, to delete the clauses authorizing civil authority to fix the maximum number of clergymen, and prohibiting clergy of foreign birth or any clergy to possess chattels or furniture. This, and his sponsoring for the presidency the Washington Ambassador, Bonilla, an educated moderate, threw his rabble Congress into the arms of Generals Obregon and Calles and Hill, who marched with commandeered Yaquis and other Sonoran recruits fully equipped with United States arms and munitions. Carranza fled, and he was shot by Obregon's henchman, General Herrero.

Calles, who was expert in getting rid of his rivals, disposed likewise of their ambitious triumvir, Hill; and naming De la Huerta temporary president, Obregon, while constitutionally disqualified, had himself, with the backing of Calles, soon counted into the presidency. He was duly recognized in Washington, though the mere accusation of the murder of his predecessor had disqualified Huerta, who was both qualified and elected constitutionally.

Roosevelt's Appraisal of Wilson's Interventions

Theodore Roosevelt's summing of the Wilsonian epoch will also apply substantially, as in most particulars, to our course in the ensuing period:

"The act of permitting the passage of arms across the frontier, on the part of Wilson, meant that he not only actively helped the insurrection, but without any doubt provided the means of achieving success, in so far as he actively prevented Huerta from organizing an effective resistance. The defenders of Wilson allege that he could not have prevented the passage of arms across the frontier. Our reply to that is: Wilson did, at times prevent such gun-running.

"He thus proved that he was actively interested in arming the revolutionists, and when he so desired, he gave permission; when he wished otherwise, he refused it; he was therefore absolutely responsible for this." (The "U. S. Foreign Relations Papers, 1914" disclose direct Bryan-Wilson activity in arming and urging the rebels.)

"And again the United States would not have had the least responsibility for what has been done to the Church, if the faction which committed these outrages had not been enabled to triumph by the United States. But since the United States took part in a civil war in Mexico, in the manner in which Wilson and Bryan obliged our government to take part, this country, through this act alone, is responsible for the horrible injustices, the terrible outrages, committed by the victorious revolutionaries against hundreds of believers of both sexes.

"Not long ago, President Wilson, in a speech delivered at Swarthmore, Pa., declared that 'In no part of this continent can any government survive that is stained with blood,' and in Mobile he said: 'We shall never forgive iniquity solely because it may be more convenient for us to do so.

"At the very moment he was pronouncing these high-sounding phrases, the leaders of the faction which he actively aided, were shooting down hundreds in cold blood; they were torturing men supposed to be wealthy; they were casting forth from their homes hundreds of peaceful families; they were sacking the churches and maltreating priests and religion in the most infamous manner, from assassination to mutilation and outrage.

"In other words, at the very time the President assured us 'That in no part of this hemisphere can any government endure if it be stained with blood,' he was helping to put in power a government that was not only stained with blood, but was stained with stains worse than those of blood. At the very time he announced, 'that he would not continue relations with iniquity even if it were more convenient to do so,' he not only consorted with iniquity, but openly supported and put in power men whose actions were those of barbarians." (New York Times, December 6, 1914.)

Roosevelt's Last Warning Still Unheeded

Theodore Roosevelt's last message to the American people contains words on the Mexican situation which are even truer now than they were then: "Mexico is our Balkan Peninsula, and during the last five years, thanks largely to Mr. Wilson's able assistance, it has been reduced to a condition as hideous as that of the Balkan Peninsula under Turkish rule. We are in honor bound to remedy this wrong."

That, in the years since the elder Roosevelt left this charge upon our honor, we have done naught to remedy but much to intensify the wrong, will be the painful burden of the remainder of this narrative.

No ruthless Mahometan ever wreaked such hideous savageries on the Christians of the Balkans as the Communists whom we have aided and abetted are now inflicting on the Christians of Mexico by totalitarian impact on mind and person and property and life.

While this diabolical persecution is most rampant, our United States Ambassador presents us to the world as aiding and abetting them now.

Thrice has he intensified the wrong by his glowing laudations of the tyrants it has made and the tyrannies on conscience it empowered them to perpetrate; and still he consorts with them complacently, unrecalled and unrebuked.

When nation-wide protest against his eulogies of Calles and of the Calles program to "take possession of the consciences of children, of youth," and of all, moved Assistant Secretary of State Phillips to inquiry, Mr. Daniels replied that he stood for the three most sacred liberties: of education, of religion, and of the press.

Deepens Conviction of U. S. Support

The Mexican papers reported that Mr. Phillips cautioned him to say nothing offensive to any section of the Mexican people and to make no further statement that could be misinterpreted. A few weeks later Mr. Daniels paid a visit of honor to the Mexican Senate on the very day on which by constitutional amendment and by statute it had destroyed the last remnant of his three sacred liberties of education, religion, and of the press; and he escaped the literal violation of Mr. Phillips' injunction by allowing his guest, Senator Reynolds of North Carolina, to pronounce the eulogies. In seeming defiance of our State Department he has since violated its instructions in letter as well as in spirit.

Meanwhile university students had raised such a united and forceful protest throughout the nation against the amendment Callesizing compulsory atheistic and sexualistic education universally, that the government was forced to exempt the universities from its present incidence; and Mr. Daniels could have witnessed, with me, the splendid delegates of twenty-four universities collaborating for a week in El Labor Building on the means and methods by which they could attain and defend liberty of religion and of education throughout Mexico.

He could, and should have witnessed the defiant parade of 10,000 students and their triumphant resistance to the attempt of Calles' police to disperse them when they denounced his educational tyranny at El Palacio Nacional. He could have seen some 60,000 parents and pupils marching in silent protest to the same National Palace despite the tear-gassing and other assaults by Calles' champions of liberty.

Outrages Mr. Daniels' Eyes Could See

Had he read Excelsior, La Palabra, El Universal, Omega, El Hombre Libre, and the other Mexico City press decreed for suppression, our Ambassador would have known that dismissal was the fate of all teachers and employees, and disqualification for all pupils, who failed to appear in the Calles parades. He surely must have known that these penalties and worse were being inflicted on all opponents or disapprovers of the

Calles plan throughout all the states of Mexico; and he could have noticed the unwillingness of the paraders that Calles drafted into blasphemous protest on the feast of Christ the King.

He knew that all private schools were closed and all but a few of God's' temples; that priests were already banned from fourteen states and many tortured or slain, and that all priests and bishops were listed for expulsion and that amendments were posted in congress demanding their death.

Mr. Daniels knew, moreover, that a noted Red Cross institution that gave free medical care to the poorest and most afflicted had been seized and suppressed because it was Catholic, and that the Mexican Bar and Medical Associations had entered unanimous protest against these and other iniquities of the Calles laws and deeds penalizing liberty and "forcing Marxian Socialism down the throats of Mexico."

Countless other evidences should have forced on him the truth of Professor Halperin's statement in **Current History**: "There is a widespread longing to dump the whole Partido Nacional Revolucionario, Calles and all, into the Gulf of Mexico. Talk to the Mexicans of the most diverse occupations in all parties of the republic and they practically are as one in denouncing 'Callismo.' " That is, that Calles was considered a curse there as well as here.

With all this in mind or within easy reach of it, Mr. Daniels paid a formal visit to Calles, who was not the official president, in his palatial residence at Cuernavaca, where, writes **El Nacional,** "The Most Excellent ambassador of the United

States greeted and conversed at length with the great chief of the revolution, General Plutarco Elias Calles."

This El Nacional, which is the official organ of the P. N. R., Calles' "National Revolutionary Party," and vilifies everything Catholic, announced November 7 that it "obtained important statements from the distinguished diplomat, who said to us: 'I consider General Calles the strong and vigorous man of Mexico. I took much pleasure in shaking hands with him.'"

Calles Organ and Daniels Exchange Eulogies

Mr. Daniels complimented the government on the commercial and financial condition of the country, and added: "Mexico is at peace; for this reason it is prospering."

Having pronounced this judgment on the general persecuting turmoil that is now rampant, its official and vilest journalistic promoter received from the "most Excellent Ambassador of the United States" special encomium and endorsement: "I take pleasure in making this statement to El Nacional, for which I have particular admiration because it knows how to interpret the sense of the Mexican revolution."

This is plainly a formal endorsement of Calles and his party, their plans, acts, proceedings, and propaganda, and fully justifies the charge of El Hombre Libre and the surviving press that Ambassador Daniels is deliberately creating the impression that the United States government is also a backer of Calles; and they are surprised, as are we, that he has not been long ago recalled. They know better than Daniels, says El Hombre

Libre, that Calles was "Mexico's strong man," for
they have felt the strength of his hands as the
Christians felt the persecuting hands of Nero and
Diocletian.

Fetes Official Persecuting Chief

In a fourth offense a few days later Mr. Dan-
iels again gave ample warrant for recall. On
November 7, the Mexico City journals printed
in English and Spanish an item that was sent
them officially by the American Embassy: "The
Ambassador of the United States of America and
Mrs. Josephus Daniels have had as their guest at
the Embassy the Governor of Puebla, General
Jose Mijares Palancia, and Senora V. de Mijares
Palancia."

On the same day El Nacional, under the cap-
tion: "General Mijares congratulated for his vigorous defanaticizing campaign by the National
Revolutionary Party," described glowingly how
the governor, going directly from the American
Embassy to Revolutionary Headquarters, reported that his campaign against the Church had extinguished fanaticism and planted communistic
culture in Puebla. He had his Puebla legislature
take further steps to break the moral pressure
exercised by priests upon the masses, and organized an intense propaganda program to that end.
This Governor Palancia is notorious throughout
Mexico as a virulent persecutor and insatiable
grafter, and a bosom friend of Calles.

The communication from the American Embassy also informed the Mexican public through
every journalistic channel that General Mijares
and company were the guests at the Symphony
Orchestra concert of Mr. and Mrs. Daniels.

President Owes Mexico a New Deal

Clearly Mr. Daniels was seizing every official and extra-official opportunity to blaze before the world and impress on the people of Mexico that our government looks with special favor on the man and the party that are robbing them of the three sacred liberties of education, religion, and the press. Surely this also is a wrong which Theodore Roosevelt would indignantly proclaim that we are in honor bound to repair.

For a century the real Mexican people have in vain been seeking a new deal of justice from the United States; and their best men will tell you, and convince you, that in short order they could put down tyranny and establish a free and just democracy, if only the giant strength of the United States would cease to intervene against them, by embargoes and treaties and force, in support of the tyrant minority, and by such supporting sanctions as the diplomatic gestures of Ambassador Josephus Daniels.

As no subsequent president has done so, it devolves on the present President Roosevelt, in whose term the "hideous" horrors have culminated, to execute the last and now more compelling behest of former President Roosevelt: "We are in honor bound to remedy this wrong."

CHAPTER VII

How We Sponsored the Calles Gang

The Men Our Ambassador Honors

THE character of the recent Mexican government may be gauged by three additions to its Cabinet: Bassols, who had to be removed in 1933 through the universal indignation aroused by his sexualization of Federal School teaching; Garrido Canabal, whose record of fanatic brutality in exterminating religion in Tabasco and demoralizing the young by lessons in obscenity, has outclassed Caligula's and Nero's; and Rodolfo Calles, the son of Putarco Calles, who expelled all priests from Sonora and likewise emulated Canabal in sex teaching monstrosities.

It was Garrido Canabal that Calles, the Supreme Chief, held up as the model of all governors, on the very day that he, Calles, announced his determination "to take possession of the consciences of the children and of youth," the phrase seized on later by Mr. Daniels to eulogize the purpose and the man. The day the atheizing educational amendment had constitutionalized the Calles plan, and its promoter proclaimed its intent to get rid of God, that "myth grotesque," and Dominguez, executive of Socialistic Education, declared the children belong altogether to the state which has the duty to free them from the superstition of religion, Mr. Daniels honored the Senate by his presence; and he journeyed later to Calles' distant palace to pronounce him "the strong man" of the Revolution and declare **El Nacional,** his journalistic organ, its authentic expression.

Not satisfied with announcing the special receptions he gave at the American Embassy to Calles' friend, the persecuting Governor of Puebla, Daniels selected for a visit of honor a still closer friend of Calles, none other than Garrido Canabal, then Minister of Agriculture.

They talked, writes **El Nacional,** about agriculture in Tabasco, possibly about the cattle show at which Canabal named the prize animals "God" and "Pope," etc., and Daniels accepted the Canabal invitation to visit Tabasco in March. No wonder the Calles organ has been pronouncing him editorially the true friend of the Revolutionary Party who, despite the pressure brought against him for his favoring acts and utterances, has retracted not a word.

Career of Calles, The Daniels Hero

Our American Ambassador's seizure of every occasion to glorify Calles and Company, and his seeming immunity therefor, become the more mysterious when we examine the record of the Supreme Chief and long the dominating force in the atheistic socialism of Mexico.

The birth record of Plutarco Elias Calles has never been produced and he has never proved his eligibility for the presidency, which the Constitution forbids to an alien or offspring of an alien parent. The reputed son of an Armenian or

Semitic father and popularly termed "The Turk,"
he is half-brother, probably by adoption, to Ar-
turo Malvido Elias, and his Elias "uncles" held
property in Sonora.

Made successively, by their influence, primary
school teacher at Guaymas and municipal treas-
urer, he was dismissed for immorality and dis-
appearance of funds. When he rose from bartend-
er to owner of the Elias hotel, the establishment
took fire under circumstances that barred him
insurance. A farm and flour mill which the Elias-
es next found for him became bankrupt; and in
1911 we find him chief of police of the frontier
town of Agua Prieta and owner of a saloon and
gambling hall, which he made the only one by
killing his rival and appropriating his goods.

Kills, Robs, Riots, But Prohibits

His patronage of brothels and seizure of women gave him unprintable nicknames. Captured
in 1912 by Escandon, a Huerta officer, he was
saved from execution by Dr. Manuel Huerta; and
Calles, when Governor of Sonora, rewarded his
savior by having him hanged with other refugees
whom he had brought forcibly from Douglas,
Arizona. This was but one of the many occasions
on which he violated American territory with
impunity.

Rising with Obregon into prominence among
the Carranza-Villa bandits of Sonora, Calles mas-
sacred and robbed, March 1, 1917, Felix Archon-
do and others who were fleeing from Villa at the
time of Pershing's pursuit of him; and he was
rewarded with the governorship of Sonora.

Though then a noted inebriate, Calles enacted

absolute prohibition under penalty of death. There is, or was, a record at the American Consulate in Hermosilla of some bottles of cognac which a friend procured there for the intoxicated Calles because the consul was the only one whom he, Calles, could not execute. That morning, Calles had six peons shot for possessing liquor. His thoroughness won him valuable favor from the prohibition sectaries of the United States.

Pre-eminently expert in disposing speedily of dangerous enemies or inconvenient friends, he rendered many such services to Obergon. The most notorious instance was his sending a gang, June 7, 1922, to murder General Lucio Blanco and Colonel Martinez who were refugees in Laredo, Texas. How they kidnapped and stabbed Blanco in American territory and threw his corpse into the Rio Grande under the written authority of Calles, is in the records at Laredo and at Washington.

United States Screens Calles' Crimes in Texas

It is not yet in the public records why Obregon, who was in collusion with the murderer of Blanco and had himself procured the murder of Carranza, was recognized by the United States in the presidency he had seized, as was Calles in succession thereto; nor why District Attorney John Valls of Laredo was debarred from arresting the author of the murder in United States territory as a result of diplomatic immunity conferred on Calles by our Secretary of State.

That there was close mutual understanding between our government and the murderous violator of our territorial rights may be gathered

from the fact that when Calles took revenge on
Judge Valls by putting Laredo under embargo
and two prominent Texas Representatives told
President Hoover that unless it was lifted at
once they would broadcast the records of the
Blanco outrage in the press, the embargo was
raised within twenty-four hours.

When, in 1923, Obregon nominated Calles to
succeed him, Adolfo de la Huerta, the popular
candidate, took the Mexican elective method of
armed opposition. His success became soon so
assured that Obregon appealed for aid to President Coolidge, who not only supplied him United States munitions and set an arms embargo
against his opponents, but gave the right of way
to his army through United States territory in
order to reach De la Huerta more conveniently.

Again U. S. Intervention Saves Calles

The **Atlantic Monthly** of July, 1927, records
that De la Huerta was conceded the election
in early December, but when on December 30,
1923, it was announced that the United States
Government had granted Obregon's request for
arms, "the significance of the sale was immediately recognized in Mexico and De la Huerta's
chances of securing foreign loans, supplies or
recognition disappeared. The morale of his forces
reflected the seriousness of the blow, for the day
the sale was announced, his was a lost cause.
* * * By its decisive intervention in the affairs of
Mexico at the end of 1923, our government, consciously or otherwise, assumed moral sponsor-
ship for the validity of the administration it
sought to enforce." This is the condition we are
in today, reached by the same methods.

Fleeing from the defeat we had procured for him, De la Huerta was hauled before United States courts, and General Estrado was cast into jail. Ten years before, President Huerta, whom we had brought to the same condition, was, though sick unto death, arrested at El Paso and thrown into a two-room shack at Fort Bliss; and the day of his burial his son-in-law, sole protector of his wife and children, was also arrested.

Huerta's dying words forgave his enemies. But the Mexicans remember; and they contrast the treatment we accorded him and the anti-Calles refugees with the immunity our government has invariably conferred upon Calles and his friends, even for crimes committed in our own territory and violations of our laws.

This is why the majority deem it hopeless to rise against their tyrants. "We feel," writes one of them, "under a powerful hand that is smashing us all"; and their only hope is that United States power will cease to sustain that tryant hand.

President Coolidge declared in 1927 that the De la Huerta revolt of 1923 would have overthrown the government had not Obregon been supplied with arms on United States credit with our consequent moral support. He made this admission because in 1927 Calles was repudiating the concessions that Obregon had made to United States mining and banking interests in order to stem the victorious armies of De La Huerta. The Republicans had been calling Wilson's Mexican policy a disgrace to our civilization, and after the Harding election in 1920 a committee was sent by Congress to investigate (Senate Resolution 106).

Perfect Precedent for Borah Resolution

Finding that under article twenty-seven of the Queretaro Constitution, the Church is stripped of property and personality and every shred of freedom, and no foreigners can exercise its ministry; that the state may filch and apportion all property at will, including buildings under American title, and bar foreigners from further acquisition, the American Committee thereon issued a truly American report (Document No. 285, 66th Congress, 2nd Session).

Having presented the facts and conditions minutely and lucidly, these representatives of the United States Foreign Relations recommended that a new treaty be drawn removing the Mexican Constitution's discriminations against American rights, or else that the United States Marines should occupy Mexican ports. They would further condition recognition on definite stipulations that Americans shall be free to enter, reside, teach, preach, and hold property in Mexico, provided they take no part in its politics, and that no retroactive laws shall apply to Americans; in brief, that the Mexican government should not be admitted to friendly relations until it had guaranteed such exercise of fundamental rights as is the wont of civilized people.

It is still more imperative that these recommendations be actualized now. The investigation by a United States Foreign Relations Committee into Mexican conditions in 1921 is a perfect precedent for the Borah Resolution of investigation into the more monstrous conditions, and more injurious to us, that prevail in 1935. These conditions make it mandatory on Senate and

Congress and people to overrule the unwarranted pressure that Secretary of State Hull has exercised to keep this Resolution shelved, and to see to it that the new investigating committee shall promptly act and that its recommendations shall not again be discarded.

Sinister influences saw to it that the wise and practical report of the 1921 committee was cast aside. Some oil magnates and other concessionary as well as sectarian interests became active, and arrangements were made with Obregon whereby the National Petroleum Oil Company should hold a 51 per cent interest in oil preserves in return for a $5,000,000 bonus, for assistance in flotation of loans, and for American recognition.

Human Rights Sacrificed to Profiteers

Messrs. Warren and Payne and other American parties to the contract, ignored the fact that Obregon had the Senate opposition leader shot and other Senators kidnapped in order to effect it. Ambassador Warren likwise ignored the murder of Mrs. Rosalie Evans and hundreds of others whose lands were coveted by the bandit "Agrarians," and the wide-spread ruin and rape, resulting in the further impoverishment of the poor and helpless, but in the millionaire enrichment of Obregon and Calles and their gang.

By 1925 twenty million acres, worth about two billion pesos, had been seized. Production fell, imports rose, prices doubled, and over a million, mostly peons, had fled to the United States.

While these were a burden on our people, the diplomatic injuries to our honor were more serious. Obregon's promise of commercial concessions had thrown the demand of the Foreign Relations Committee for a guarantee of fundamental rights completely into the discard. On September 23, 1923, President Coolidge granted full recognition to the Obregon regime; and when a few months later Obregon was hard pressed by De la Huerta, his American Oil beneficiaries were able to secure for him Washington's saving intervention. Another candidate, General Flores of Sinaloa, was also making headway, but Calles was able unaided to attend to that. Flores died of poison before the "election" was selected.

But when Calles was counted into the presidency he had his judges reverse their reversal of the Constitution regarding the petroleum concessions, and he proclaimed immediate enforcement of both its anti-religious and confiscatory provisions. He had made Morones, who headed his personal political faction disguised as a labor union, Secretary of Commerce, and through him procured the support of the American Federation of Labor; and as a Thirty-third Degree Mason he counted on the backing of American Masonry through the Supreme Council of the Scottish Rite which had just voted him the medal of highest Masonic distinction.

How Calles Played Up to U. S. Sects

Though hating all Religion, Calles found it politic then to keep the American sects on his side. Notorious for affording friendly facilities to Protestant proselyters and frequently supplying them with temples and institutions of the Church that he was ruthlessly persecuting, Calles won enthusiastic support from the Baptist and Methodist and Protestant alliance, and anti-Saloon League, and the then pervasive Ku Klux Klan. It may be noted here that the Methodist convention at Birmingham, December, 1933, acclaimed a resolution commending the Daniels defense of Mexico's religious persecutors, though they have lost the political control of their membership that Mr. Daniels' friend, Bishop Cannon, once exercised.

Hence, while postponing confiscation of American properties for the moment, Calles continued recklessly the expulsion of foreign as well as native priests and religious, including Archbishop Caruana, Papal Delegate and American citizen, and extended nation-wide confiscation and spoliation of churches and religious institutions, with accompaniments of murder, desecration, rape, and other crimes and unprintable brutalities, that cover hundreds of pages in the records.

The more effectually to crush resistance, he issued June 14, 1926, supplementary decrees, so clamping down the 1917 Constitution that no religious institution may exist, no religious service may be held in family or home, and within the tolerated churches no priests may function except such as the state permits and in the manner, measure, times, places, and numbers the state prescribes. Aided effectively by Morones, he had these decrees executed with a brutal relentlessness that spared neither sex nor sanctuary nor cloister; and persons as well as all seizable properties were ravished.

Bishop Manriquez Arouses Mexico's Manhood

Then something new happened in Mexico. Living under the sword or the threat of it for a century, Bishops and clergy had come to accept persecution without protest and welcome the slightest toleration as a gift; but in 1926 Bishop Manriquez of Huejutla issued a pastoral that was unique in Mexican allocutions.

Painting the outrages on human rights that the Calles hyper-Jacobinism inflicts and the suicide which the Church's submission to State license for every act of ministry and worship and even of expression had involved, Bishop Manriquez summoned priests and people to defend their rights against this fury of outrage on their faith and manhood. Their failure therein was the source of their calamities. Not only was it an obvious lie that the Church had played politics; it was their culpable omission to take civic action on the principles and problems of good government for the welfare of their people that had brought on them God's anger of which their persecutors are but the instruments.

Let them repair the omission; assert their citizenship; resist the destroyers of human rights, stand steadfast nor flee before the wolf; be martyrs, if need be, for faith and freedom and go boldly to prison and to death. Let pastors set examples of sacrifice to their flocks. If churches are closed make every home a sanctuary. If one school is seized, open another; and hold school under tents and trees if roofs be barred. By sacrifice of pleasure, by Christian virility, let young and old, but the young men foremost, fight God's battle; and never yield nor falter till every manacle of religion, education, and civic freedom be struck from Constitution and law. Thus will God lift His chastisement for their culpable suf-

france of wrong and bring them from the cata-
combs to the sun of liberty.

Bishop Manriquez Tortured by "Law"

The imprisonment and cruel torture of the
brave Bishop Manriquez burned his appeal into
the heart of Mexico. The pleadings of Archbishop
Mora, the ranking prelate, for the "liberty of conscience of thought, of worship, of teaching, association and of press that is the right of Christians,
of citizens, and of man" had been summarily
rejected by Calles in almost the words demanding Christ's death of Pilate: "We have a law."

Then, as now, Calles had his agents proclaim
through the United States that these laws, which
penalize every form of Christian worship and
right, and force Communist atheism and ethics
on the youthful mind, are measures of enlightened
social reform against clerical reactionaries. Petitions against them of over two millions of voting
age, showing the true mind of the Mexican people, were thrown out by his Congress without
discussion, and Calles proceeded to confiscate
schools, churches, convents, and hospitals, casting priests, sisters, and religious on the streets,
often with accompaniment of murder and rape.

To give plausible color to this propaganda,
Calles was careful to protect the persons and temples of non-Catholic ministers and of the less than
a dozen priests who yielded to his laws; but he
had all others of foreign birth deported, including
Mother Semple of the Visitation convent and
many other Americans whose character and services shed lustre on their country.

Coolidge Government Ignored All Outrages

President Coolidge and Secretary Kellogg, who quickly secured redress from Calles for his tampering with American banking and mining interests by threatening an embargo, took no notice of these outrages; and Mr. Kellogg coldly informed the United States Episcopate that he had handed over their protest to the Mexican Consulate, Calles' principal agency for mendacious propaganda. Outrages on the religious and most fundamental rights, even of his own nationals, was merely an internal affair beyond his competency; but violation of properties was a crime against international law.

Shorn of all hope from their own government and from ours, the Mexican people hearkened to the call of Bishop Manriquez with a heroism worthy of his own. Declaring acceptance of the Calles decrees apostacy, the Mexican Episcopate ordered suspension of Church services, July 31, 1926, the date of their enforcement; and the young men and women of Mexico, forming a well-knit League of Religious Liberty, struck a practical blow at their tyrants by an intensive boycott on luxuries and the articles yielding them heaviest taxation. A fifty per cent fall in revenue within the year was another proof of the hostility of the Mexican people to their armed minority Government, and also of their manhood in sacrificial devotion to Religion and Liberty.

They were to prove it by severer tests. Shot down or cast into foul dungeons, their leaders were promptly replaced by others equally effective, and Attorney General Ortega resorted to

the foul device of outraging and formally order-
ing the penalty of outrage on the active young
ladies of the League. It was such outrages on
their women, accompanied by sacrilegious outrages on their priests and sanctuaries, that moved the unarmed fathers and sons and brothers to
seize arms where they could and rise in revolt.

Revolt Against Sacrilege, Rape, and Rapine

When General Ortiz and federal forces shot
down Father Batiz and four laymen in Zacatecas,
desecrated the sanctuary, and raped the women
of Valparaiso, Pedro Quintinar gathered his
neighbors together and extinguished the miscreants to a man. Thus started the Cristero revolt, which spread from State to State with like
spontaneity.

That the ensuing fight for liberty under the
slogan, Viva Cristo Rey, was as heroic as
history records will appear in our sketch of the
1926-1929 period. It was distinctively a lay movement. The Bishops' conciliating policy had failed. They had been exiled or jailed, and hundreds
of priests had been slain or hunted like felons.

Out of over 4,000 priests only ten are known
to have taken Calles' bribe of high pay and lux-
urious living for joining his "National Church."
Instead, the priests suffered poverty, hunger, and
banishment, and often torture and death. But
few of them, and much less the Episcopate, encouraged recourse to arms. It was the Calles
outrages that goaded the laity into what seemed
hopeless resistance.

History repeats itself. A few of the like outrages of today have got into our papers. Indians,

women as well as men, guarding their Church
with folded arms in Chiapas, were shot down by
the State soldiery. The Red Shirts of Cabinet
Minister Canabal outraged many church services
and shot down attendants at Mass in Coyoacan.
In another suburb of their capital, the police,
January 12, "stormed a little church," leaving
worshippers dying and dead; and Mayor Aaron
Saenz put the blame on the people for flagrant
violation of the law against church-going. Five
thousand students who assembled in unarmed
protest at the Red Shirts' headquarters were
likewise attacked. These are but a few of the
outrages that accompany the enforcement of
decrees against law and liberty and the funda-
mentals of all decencies of civilization.

People Fought For Rights

Nor are the rapings and torturings of the Cristero period missing. Bishop Manriquez has written from his enforced exile in San Antonio that
the man who will defend his mother with naked
fists will even so avenge the sacrilegious violation of his religion, the Mother of all Sanctities.

Archbishop Ruiz, Apostolic Delegate, has issued a Pastoral declaring that the Bishops will
not interfere with the people's forcible defense of
their rights, either promoting or prohibiting.
Shall we stand by without protest while our
brethren are being goaded into fighting for their
liberties with naked fists? Shall we again permit
our Government to see to it that the fists of
Mexican defenders of Religious Liberty and Human Rights be naked in the fight, and to arm and
armor the fists of their oppressors while keeping
Mr. Daniels to hearten them with his favors?

Shall we allow the Supreme Masonic Councils, which both in the United States and Mexico by address and cable and influence vindicated the Calles policies before, to dominate our Government again?

Though such questions have been addressed, directly or by implication, to the President and Secretary of State by numerous societies and multitudes of citizens, they have elicited no assurance of redress. Replying to the repeated insistencies of Supreme Knight Carmody, in behalf of half a million Knights of Columbus and millions of other citizens, that he cease to intervene for Mexico's tyrants and act good neighbor to its people, President Roosevelt affirmed, clearly if ingenuously, that, reverting the policy of his predecessors towards other oppressed peoples, he would take no action against whatsoever abominations Mexico's government should wreak, even upon our own nationals in its territory.

This makes it incumbent on all patriotic citizens to uphold the Knights of Columbus in directing their government servants to restore American justice, and to execute now the last behest of Theodore Roosevelt: "We are in honor bound to remedy this wrong."

CHAPTER VIII

U. S. Parleys Nullified Cristero Heroism

Cardenas Vindicates Canabal's Murderers

PRESIDENT Cardenas, having decreed rigid enforcement of the Calles atheizing program, issued a pronouncement on the assaulting and shooting of peaceful worshippers by the Canabal Red Shirts at Coyoacan and by his own police at Tacubaya, in the Federal District. He had the audacity to say that the "clerical group" had incited these "riots," and thus got themselves attacked and slaughtered in order "to embarrass the government." Hence such meetings shall be held no more, unless in buildings at their own disposal when legally authorized.

But since these meetings were services in their own churches, and any religious meeting now renders the edifice wherein it is held the property of the State, one can see what a mockery is this statement, issued for United States consumption. He put no restrictions on the Red Shirts, who met where they pleased by Canabal's direction, usually in front of a church, shouting foul tirades against everything holy.

In fact, all Christian meetings, whether in or out of Church, are already prohibited by the constitutional and statutory enactments recently perfected by Calles' National Revolutionary Party.

It is a complete commentary on the unnatural barbarity of these "laws" that they gave full legal authorization to Mayor Aaron Saenz for having his police shoot down the Tacubaya Congregation and their sympathizing neighbors, and for pronouncing the resistance of the worshippers rebellion. It is legalized murder on a nationwide scale. The same principle was applied to the wanton destruction of the property as well as person of "fanatics," when on January 7 a group of Red Shirts was discovered setting fire to the altar of the City Church of Santa Catarina after pillaging the edifice.

Commissioner Martinez was likewise legally correct in discharging the miscreants, on the ground that the embarrassment the defending populace had caused them was punishment enough. The blasphemous outraging and shooting of the Coyoacan worshippers and the firing upon the 6,000 protesting students at the Red Shirt headquarters were irregular in that the assailants followed general orders rather than specific; but this was quickly rectified by the chief of the Red Shirts, Garrido Canabal, whose dismissal from the Cabinet the students had demanded in the public theater and in addresses before the presidential palace.

Canabal Sovietized The "Reign of Terror"

Cabinet Minister Canabal, whose nephew was captain of the Red Shirt assassins, had the leader set free at once and ultimately the whole party of sixty, transferring the guilt to their victims; and though a professed prohibitionist, he supplied them champagne to drink to their deed.

Meanwhile he organized an atheistic course for all his employes in the Palace of Fine Arts. His courses included the de-religionizing texts and naked sex teaching he had established at Tabasco, and he compelled every employe to purchase two notoriously atheistic and immoral productions as essential to their training. He had them all initiated in his Masonic Lodge, exhorting them to unite with all Masonry in "crushing the brute rock of the heads of the fanatics."

On Saturday, December 8, Feast of the Immaculate Conception, he compelled his initiates to celebrate the first Sabado Rojo or Red Saturday in Hidalgo Theater, rehearsing them in the works and ways of "defanaticizing" according to the Red "National Calendar" he has devised to replace the Christian calendar, thus repeating the achievement of a reign of terror in France. Secretary Telles issued like orders, and Cardenas has confirmed publicly these copyings of Canabal and Bassolls and the younger Calles. In fact, this Minister of Agriculture was running all Cabinet procedure by the methods as well as motives of his Tabasco atheizations, and has thus made the government of Mexico a still more brutally systematized instrument to de-religionize and demoralize its people.

Our Ambassador Compliments Canabal

It was after these manifestations had been largely discussed, and were praised or condemned in the revolutionary and independent journals, that the United States Ambassador paid Garrido Canabal the visit of friendly courtesy, which the Calles organ El Nacional held up to the nation

as further proof of the unbroken support and
sympathy yielded to the Mexican government at
its Reddest by Mr. Daniels, and, consequently,
by the United States government he represents.

The chief of our State Department's Mexican
division has informed the writer that Mr.
Daniels paid a like visit to all the members of the
Cabinet, and President Roosevelt has since repeated this, the only extenuation presented. It
but multiplies the offense. Custom does not re-
quire Ambassadors to call on every Cabinet Minister. Besides, in profession and practice they
were all of the same ilk, from President Cardenas
down; and diplomatic etiquette demands no such
refinement of courtesy to ministers whose tyran-
nic system of government is an absolute negation
of our fundamental principles, and whose brutal
uprooting of civil and religious liberty is a stink
in the nostrils of humanity.

It has been said in further extenuation that
Mr. Daniels is ignorant of Spanish. How is it
that his ignorance puts him always on the side
of the persecutors? He has assistants who have
knowledge of Spanish. If he is unable to get
himself informed that his actions and utterances
are such as to convince the Mexican people that
the United States is their enemy, then he is unfit
to represent a civilized nation; and if, on either
ground, he is not recalled, we shall have confirmed the convictions of the Mexican majority
that the present ruthless assault on their liberties, civil and religious, and on the very minds
and souls of their children, are sustained by the
government of Ambassador Daniels.

U. S. Share In Calles-Canabal Outrages

We should also have to share the responsibility for the casualties and disasters that such provocations must necessarily evoke. It was similar persecutions that incited the Cristero revolt of 1926-29, and it was the same persecutors that perpetrated or caused the murders and killings and wanton destructions of that period.

The provocation was inaugurated by the same Garrido Canabal, who in 1925 decreed that only married clergymen, and but seven of these, could minister in Tabasco. Though charged with murder, rape, robbery, and other crimes manifold and specific, Garrido was resolutely sustained by Calles; and other governors followed his example in expelling priests and sisterhoods with brutal maltreatment and seizing and despoiling churches and institutions. It was then Bishop Manriquez was imprisoned for his manful protest, and the venerable Archbishop Mora of Mexico City was deported, with five other prelates, February 19, 1926, merely for stating that episcopate and clergy and people would continue to combat those articles and decrees that abrogate religion and proscribe the natural rights of man.

Archbishop Ruiz' account of their encounter with Tejeda, Calles' Secretary of the Interior, who had summoned them from their place of detention, is instructive.

Archbishop Mora Answers Tyrant

Announcing that by the President's orders they must leave the country overnight, he said their approval by silence of the Archbishop of Durango's pastoral, justifying the Catholic laity for taking arms in self-defense, constituted them rebels and leaders of rebellion. Archbishop Mora replied: "Sir, the Episcopate has prompted no revolution. It has, however, declared the immemorial right of laymen to defend by force the natural rights they could not by peaceful means protect."

"That," said Tejeda, "is rebellion against legal authority." "It is no rebellion," was the answer. "It is self-defense against unjustifiable tyranny. As for authority, the world knows the illegality of the elections that brought you to power."

Congress had already decreed forfeiture of citizenship against the bishops for petitioning to amend the laws and, by implication, against the two million signatories to the same petition. Now, they were also guilty of treason, for, announced the Minister: "The agitation of these gentlemen against the government constitutes them rebels," and, hence, directly subjected to the executive penalty for treason. Tejeda had qualified for the Cabinet, as had Canabal in Tabasco, by expulsion of priests and religious in Guadalajara, and by forcing such teachings on schools as his mock baptisms of groups of boys and girls of 15, stripped naked for the purpose, would suggest.

The expulsion of all the bishops he could reach was but the prelude or pretext for the launching of Calles' determined plan of universal persecution, just as a like protest by Archbishop Ruiz and Bishop Manriquez have been made the pretext for recent more intensive persecution. The general opposition of the people was as manifest then as it is now. Over three thousand parishioners made strenuous resistance to the closing

of the Holy Family Church in Mexico City. Some
six hundred girls in the Teresan Sisters' School
barricaded themselves in the institution when
their teachers were thrown into the street, and
held it for five days foodless, surrendering only
on the pledge, which was promptly broken, that
the Sisters would be restored to them.

People's Hatred Of Mexican Tyrants

These instances, as well as the general and
often fierce resistance in the recent outrages at
Coyoacan and Tacubaya and Santa Catalina, and
in numerous churches and congregations elsewhere, make two things manifest: First, that the
vast majority of the Mexican people are not only
unsympathetic, but absolutely antagonistic to the
tyranny that rules them; and second, that they
are a true and brave people ready to suffer and
combat for their religion and their liberties, even
with "naked fists." This they did in 1926-1929,
with the hopeless heroism which we shall outline
in the hope that our government and people shall
not again favor the forces of tyranny, but rather
shall take salutary measures to prevent such
another disastrous struggle as the present symp-
toms would indicate is imminent.

Even before Calles had rejected Archbishop
Mora's demand of "A free Church in a free State"
and his Congress had flouted the petition therefor of two million voters, the goading persecutions had begun. In Colima, San Luis Potosi,
Michoacan, Durango, Guanajuato, Jalisco, peaceful civilians as well as priests were attacked, tortured, and slaughtered by federal officers, who
were sustained in every instance by the military

chief, even when burnings, robberies, and rapings were superadded.

It was most of all the planned and sanctioned criminal outrages on girls and women, which Pius XI denounced, November 18, 1926, that drove the men to arms in desperate defense. Within a year 146 priests and countless peaceful civilians, including youths of both sexes, were murdered, often after incredible torture and outrage, in pursuance of the Calles campaign. It was Calles who created the Cristeros.

The Great Cristero Uprising, 1926-1929

The uprisings consisted at first of unconnected groups which sprang up spontaneously in the localities that were outraged by the Federal detachments let loose through the land. As the multiplication and barbarity of the outrages multiplied, the revolting sections unified and the League of Religious Liberty, whose leaders knew nothing of warfare, assumed direction.

They sent two brilliant young men of high character and connections to secure arms and support in the United States; but the more effective of these was arrested here for conspiracy against a friendly government and sentenced to two years' imprisonment by our Federal Courts; and they found, moreover, that such activities were regarded unfavorably here by not a few people of influence as "fomenting rebellion" with a neighboring country recognized by ours.

Then the Cristeros, hopeless of external aid, united under a soldier of transcendent ability; and, thrown on their own resources, they made a fight, which though little known abroad, is still

ringing through Mexico and inciting like resistance to today's deadlier persecuting outrages.
Centred in the most populous states of Michoacan, Guanajuato and Jalisco, which, being also
the richest, had suffered most from Federal outrages on property and person, the Cristeros soon
had all but the larger cities in their hands.

Heroines of Joan of Arc Brigades

Getting arms and supplies by raiding barracks
and ambushing troops and rifling the express,
they lived on donations of the poor, which their
sisters and daughters carried on horseback to the
mountains. These, the "Brigades of Saint Joan
of Arc," were worthy of their patroness. They
gathered arms and munitions wherever they
could be bought or taken, often from the Calles
soldiery, they manufactured bombs, and rode
long and perilous distances to carry them, with
news of the enemy movements, to the camps of
their fighting kin. Many were captured, and the
invariable outrages that followed but strengthened and spurred to further heroism the Joan of
Arc brigades through Mexico. One of them, a
young lady from Tabasco, told me how they still
supply arms to the protectors of the priests
hunted down by Garrido Canabal, and she added
proudly: "We are no cowards in Tabasco."

That word could be extended far and wide in
Mexico, but with special emphasis in Jalisco.
Dissuaded by Archbishop Orozco, who while opposing revolt never condemned the revolters and
is still hiding and hunted with his people, the
Jaliscans were the last to rise; but they were
foremost then, and they have not yielded yet.

Their lay leader, Gonzales Flores, though agreeing with the Archbishop that without arms the fight was hopeless, took command of his no longer restrainable people; but soon he was captured, and the Callistas prolonged his execution with public torturings, deeming this would terrorize Jalisco. It had the opposite effect. Though at this juncture the United States administration had renewed its friendship with Calles and the Cristero's reliance on other aid had proved illusory, thus precluding all hope of arms or help from without, the brave Jaliscans not only kept up the fight but widened the area of battle. The brutalities to Flores summoned to them a leader who welded the Cristeros of a dozen states into a disciplined national army that seriously threatened the supremacy of Calles.

Exiled as an officer of Huerta who had routed the Villa-Carranza wreckers at Torreon, Enrique Gorostieta recrossed the Rio Grande in 1927, and, elected to succeed the murdered Flores, he had organized within a year a disciplined army of twenty thousand men in a dozen states, and in 1929 had as many more in formation.

Callista Savageries Stimulate Cristeros

Avoiding pitched battles, and distributing contingents over a wide territory, he directed them when and where to attack, and how to lure the opposing forces to the mountains and, with the expert assistance of the Joan of Arc brigades, to get arms and munitions from the enemy. Soon he had the great central states cleared of the government garrisons, and treble the number of its hired forces would fly from the onslaught of his trained and eager volunteers.

The welcome and aid everywhere accorded
him is largely accounted for by the conduct of
the Calles troops. Typical of hundreds of recorded instances was the tearing out of the
tongues of unarmed youths at Leon before execution, because, when lined up to be shot, they
cried in unison, "Viva Cristo Rey." Other prominent young men at Angel had the skin pulled
off their heads and fingers for similar witness to
Christ the King before being butchered; and
General Flores and his captured companions
were hung up by the thumbs while their flesh
was slashed with razors.

The multiplication of such savageries, with
the general burnings and rapings that marked
the march of the Callistas, instead of terrorizing
stimulated the Cristeros to fiercer reprisals, until
expedition after expedition was harried, decim-
ated, driven out, or exterminated. The outrages
on villages and ranches had raised the entire
populace against Calles in defense of their lands
and homes, so that soon the insurrection became
a national rather than a religious movement
under the battle cry, "Dios, Patria, Libertad"
(God, Fatherland, Liberty).

Calles' Baffled Armies Multiply Barbarities

The situation for the Mexican Government had
become so menacing that the Secretary of War,
General Amaro, took the field himself with a
large force of infantry, artillery, and cavalry.
Months of campaigning in the mountains, into
which Gorostieta skilfully lured him, cut his
troops in half and supplied plentiful munition to
the enemy; and he returned, after much destruc-

tion of civilian properties and persons, without gaining a foot of ground or a single victory.

Other military chiefs, who were sent to repel the widening assaults of the Cristeros, had no better fortune. Before the end of 1927 General Gorostieta was dominating half of Mexico; and in 1928 the government was constrained to mobilize the police and the presidential guards and levy new forces to replace casualties and desertions.

Orders were issued, April 27, 1927, that all families in the regions of insurrection must concentrate in designated cities within ten days, after which the entire district would be bombarded by airplanes and destroyed. This was done. Villages were shelled and bombed, and thousands lay dead in the embers of their homes, while many of the larger thousands that fled to the cities were shot down on the way or died of famine and pestilence.

Raping, as usual, was added to these horrors, which, instead of subduing, stimulated further the high spirit of Jalisco, supplying everywhere new recruits for Gorostieta, whose discipline included respect and protection for property and person. In May, 1929, he reported twelve victorious engagements in widely separated districts, noting valuable ammunition acquired.

At this time General Escobar, who had served Calles and Obregon by slaying their opposing candidates, Gomez and Serrano, revolted with other generals against the nomination of Portes Gil for the presidency; and he had won the battle of Jimenez, inflicting 4,000 casualties on the Calles forces, when American combat planes threw tons of asphyxiating gas bombs and incendiary grenades on the rebel troops and converted victory into rout. Again Calles was saved from inevitable defeat by timely assistance from Washington, and this "Yanqui Victory," as it was termed in Mexico, is still bitterly remembered.

Cristero Victories Imperil Calles

Though Gorostieta favored the Escobar party on the ground that "your enemy's enemy is your friend," he held his own forces apart from it, and continued his guerilla attacks on separate contingents as incessantly and successfully as before. But when Calles mobilized all his forces, including the "Agrarian" army of Morones, with the announced decision to exterminate "the fanatics," the commander changed his tactics.

As soon as General Cedillo, who was sent with 7,000 men, mostly "Agrarians," against the Cristero center in Jalisco, had divided his forces into two columns, Gorostieta, with less than a thousand men, put both successively to rout in open onslaught, capturing all their artillery, arms, and supplies. The surviving "Agrarians" deserted, but a sorry remnant returning to Mexico; and it is worth noting here that Cedillo retains more respect for his vanquishers than for his "Agrarian" runaways. Till his present succession to Canabal as Secretary of Agriculture, Cedillo was Governor of San Luis Potosi, the only state where religious schools are free and priests are unmolested; and for this both he and General Almazan were recently denounced by Garrido Canabal as "false Callistas."

In the spring of 1929 Gorostieta and his now seasoned fighters for "God, Fatherland, Liberty", had become a grave menace to Calles and Callismo. They were awaiting the arrival of a ship laden with ammunition, the first such consignment from abroad, to start a new offensive, and Calles was reduced to desperate straits in the capital by depleted finances and the general revulsion that his predatory policies and his persecuting cruelties had created.

Calles Saved Again by U. S. Diplomacy

At this critical moment, when the friendliness or even neutrality of our administration would have turned the scales in their favor, the defenders of religion and liberty were again overthrown by United States support of their persecuting foes; and—what was their sorest blow—with the active, if unwitting, cooperation of their own coreligionists.

The thousands of Mexico's best citizens, including bishops, priests, religious, and other hunted refugees from ruthless persecution that were cast penniless upon our shores in 1926, excited sympathy with the sufferers and general indignation against the persecutors; but it was not until the Archbishop of Baltimore put specifically the responsibility where it belonged that protest took organized form.

Finding that our administration invariably supported the red rulers of Mexico and private appeals had proved fruitless, he exposed the naked facts in **The Baltimore Catholic Review**, detailing with names and dates, how we bartered the natural rights of men for oil and money and

minerals, and condoned brutal persecution to
gratify bigotry and greed. He demanded as a
citizen, not that we intervene in behalf of the
persecuted, but that we cease to intervene against
them; that, reversing a policy as unjust as un-
American, we conduct our relations with Mexico
on the American principles of justice and of sympathy to the oppressed.

The K. of C. Campaign

In support of these indictments the Knights
of Columbus took decisive action at their Supreme Convention in Philadelphia, August 6,
1926. Centering the attention of the Order on
the rabid anti-religious persecutions of their
suffering brothers in Mexico, Supreme Knight
Flaherty said, in part: "We see their most sacred
rights abrogated or restricted; we see them vis-
ited with trials of the most cunning and vicious
conception, and we are told that this persecution
is the privilege of an independent State and are
bidden to hold our peace. . . . In the name of
humanity and liberty, we shall raise our voices
against this persecution of our brothers; even
as we would raise our voices against similar persecution wherever it might be. It is a sorry hour
for our civilization when a persecution communistic in origin, anti-religions in principle, can be
conducted under the sanction of silence. . . . We
here and now protest against it with all our
strength and determination."

Accordingly, a militant resolution was adopted
protesting the inhuman persecutions in Mexico
by a Government of Communist purposes, pre-
cept, and practice; and, pointing to the patronage

bestowed on it by the United States Government which had given aid and countenance to the Bolshevist forces of Carranza, Obregon, and Calles, it warned the American people that they could not with impunity permit a Government of Soviet philosophy at their doors that was working drastically to degrade and destroy marriage and family and reduce God and religion to a myth.

The groundless charge, which is still insistently revived against all facts and protests and was recently repeated by President Roosevelt, that the Knights had demanded United States intervention in Mexico, was refuted in official statements from their headquarters showing that the resolution made no such demand, but did point to the persecuting tyrannies in Mexico and charged these to "the recognition accorded its Communistic regimes" and to "INTERVENTION BY AMERICAN EXECUTIVE AUTHORITY." In proof of this were instanced the aid and support, already recounted in this volume, which our successive administrations afforded to Carranza and Obregon by armies and navies, by sale of arms and munitions, by free transic to their armies through our territory, and by "placing an embargo on the sale and delivery of arms and munitions of war to any other than the Mexican Government itself."

Though Mr. Flaherty declined to determine for our Government what steps it should take, COLUMBIA, the official K. of C. organ, made this very clear positively and negatively: "The Knights of Columbus do not urge intervention in Mexico. They urge, rather, that the continued intervention by our Government since December 31, 1923 shall cease." Pointing again to the numerous interventions cited above, and insisting that they asked no favors for Catholic Mexico, it concluded with a statement equally descriptive of their present position: "The Knights of Columbus asked merely, and asked with full right, that the Government cease from all forms of intervention in Mexico in behalf of the Mexican enemies of religion and political freedom and private property and, ultimately, of the United States."

The Knights raised a million dollar fund, and conducted a nation-wide campaign of enlightenment on Mexican conditions and relations through public meetings and distribution of apposite literature. The campaign ended when Church authorities had accepted plausible assurances from President Coolidge and Secretary Kellog, who had just effected a satisfying compact with Calles on material American interests. But the agreement reached on Catholic interests had no such satisfying value. Rather have both agreements been utilized by Calles, and with even more ruthless efficiency by Cardenas, to instrument more drastic programs for the extinction of liberty today.

Assured of the all-powerful support of Ambasador Daniels, who has been turning his eulogies from Calles to Cardenas with easy eloquence, the present despot is extinguishing liberty with even more ruthless efficiency. This we can quickly end by exacting curt recall of the presumptive symbol of our sympathies.

CHAPTER IX

How Our New Diplomacy Empowered Calles

THE first effect of the Washington agreements of 1927 that hushed Catholic protest in the United States, was the replacement of Ambassador Sheffield by Mr. Dwight Morrow. This, the Mexican people considered unfortunate then and deem a calamity now. With the possible exception of Messrs. Lane Wilson and O'Shaughnessy, Mr. Sheffield was the outstanding American representative who won the complete confidence of the Mexican people. It is a revealing fact that Washington recalled all three.

Mr. Sheffield protested vigorously and effectively against the actual and legislative confiscations of American properties; but his honesty incurred the enmity of our banking profiteers, and he also exercised all the influence of his office in protection of civil and religious rights against Calles' persecuting policies. For this he become **persona non grata,** and for this he was recalled. Calles' way of achieving this triumph will throw some light on the favor he has maintained with successive administrations, and perhaps explain why Mr. Daniels still holds his position.

The workings of the banking corporations he had offended for an agent of their own choosing were strengthened immensely by petitions against Ambassador Sheffield that had been pouring into Washington at the rate of 800 a day. Coming from the Masonic lodges and from head-quarters of the various sects and anti-saloon leagues at the height of their political power, the protests bore the mark of careful organization in Mexico and here.

Why Mr. Morrow Replaced Mr. Sheffield

Inspired and directed by the Calles agencies, these sources could supply when desired an immense mass of petitions representing millions who knew nothing of what it was about. They broadcasted also the publicity texts: that Calles was not persecuting religion; that he was but maintaining the laws of the land; that he was giving the Protestant ministers and churches every liberty; that he supported the sacred cause of prohibition; and that he was a true and trusted Mason.

This last was the most important. The Washington Supreme Council Thirty-third Degree could, though quite unwarranted, have itself counted for three million American Masons; which, with the united Mexican Masonry and the millions claimed by the ministerial leagues, would, in the complete cessation of Catholic counteraction, make their contention seemingly unanimous. Hence Mr. Sheffield, the friend of liberty and justice, was speedily replaced by an Ambassador as acceptable to the Calles clique as to ministers and Masons and interested bankers. Our further compliance with their requirements elicited this cable to President Coolidge, August 25, 1927, from Grand Commander Rojas, of Mexico:

"In the name of the Supreme Council of the Ancient and Accepted Scottish Rite of this nation and of Mexican Masonry in general, we hereby send you our most hearty applause, and present our sincere recognition, for your firm stand in refusing to participate in any manner in the so-called Mexican religious conflict, as President of that great Republic, regardless of the pressure brought to bear upon your government for that purpose. . . . The only way to maintain public order is to enforce the laws and compel the Roman Catholic clergy to submit unconditionally to the will of the people as expressed in its Constitution."

Masonic Councils Laud Morrow and Daniels

This is also the gist of both Supreme Councils' present eulogies of Ambassador Daniels. In the same August, 1927, the New Age, organ of Supreme Council Thirty-third Degree, had a supporting article to the same effect, endorsing on behalf of American Masonry this unsanctioned "Constitution" which penalizes both religion and clergy, and robs them of legal personality. It is time that the more than ninetenths of American Masons, who are Americans first and uphold religious liberty for all, should repudiate the unwarranted assumption that they are backing religious slavery in Mexico.

The Calles publicity and other interested agencies have given Mr. Morrow a reputation in the United States quite different from that he bears in Mexico. American residents as well as the anti-Calles leaders and people are unanimous in pronouncing him the most effective agent for

the Calles interests and the most friendly to the
persecuting faction that ever represented the
United States. His banking and business experience facilitated his settlement of debt and
property claims; but qualified American residents confirm another charge of general acceptance, that he was a boon companion of Calles
and Morones in their private celebrations. However this may be, one instance alone of his public association with Calles in persecution at its
worst, killed all confidence in Mr. Morrow and all
hope of aid from the government he represented.

Fr. Pro's Murder Climaxed Calles' Butcheries

Coincident with Mr. Morrow's arrival in
Mexico, the reign of terror was at its height, and
continued unabated. I have pictures before me
of hundreds of young men and priests and even
girls, who were seized without charge and executed without trial, often with prolonged and
excruciating tortures. In the summer and fall
of 1927 indiscriminate shootings and hangings
and torturings of suspected friends of the Cristeros were multiplied, with the view of terrorizing the armed forces of revolt. These and the
murder of scores of the worthiest priests, and
the barbarous maiming and torturing of Fathers
Batiz and Reyes and other widely venerated
pastors had the contrary effect, of inflaming and
swelling the ranks of the Cristeros.

But there was one young priest whose assassination stirred public feeling most and who is
now venerated as the "Martyr of Mexico." This
was Father Miguel Augustin Pro, a young Jesuit
whose cheerful sanctity and zeal and his adept-

ness in reaching all classes with his ministry and evading the pursuivants on his track made him universally beloved as a saint and a hero.

But his marvelous feats in foiling the suppressors of Catholic worship had marked him for government vengeance. Seized on the obviously false pretext of connection with an assault upon Obregon, he was shot down November 23, 1927, without charge or trial; and he died as he had lived with a smile upon his face, forgiving cheerfully and praying heartily for the executioners of himself and his brother and fellow victims.

His sisters and his aged father dipped their kerchiefs in his blood and departed joyously; and despite the Calles soldiery, hundreds of thousands crowded to his obsequies, struggling for a relic of the martyr. The gathering masses on the streets obstructed the passage of the presidential automobile, in which, beside Plutarco Calles, the American Ambassador was seated.

Morrow Tours With Fr. Pro's Murderer

Failing even to acknowledge a legal protest submitted to him by a lawyer's committee, Mr. Morrow hastened to tour the country with Calles, who gaily played Toreador to amuse his friend. He thus impressed the world that all was well with Mexico, and made it clear to his own people and the Cristeros that even in the savagest excesses of persecution, the United States Government stood back of him. It is precisely the same despairing realization that oppresses them now when they see our Ambassador Daniels also go out of his way to show friendliest courtesies to the same or the like persecutors today and to eu-

logize the same Plutarco Calles, after the latter
had forged and had wielded a deadlier weapon
to assassinate the souls of their children.

While Mr. Morrow's friendly services were securing arms and countenance from our government for Calles, and holding strict embargo
against the League of Liberty, the Cristeros, as
we have seen, managed somehow to make headway, though with slight ecclesiastical encouragement. It was only in the face of relentless universal persecution, after millions of petitions had
been scouted and, thirty thousand injunction
protests had been overruled en masse, that re-
luctantly the bishops tolerated recourse to arms.
But Archbishop Mora, the Mexican Primate, was
exiled for defending manfully before Calles the
fighters for liberty; and Archbishop Gonzales
Valencia of Durango, who still stands by the
fighters for liberty, had heartened the belligerents
by his Pastoral from Rome, February 11, 1927.

Expressing veneration for his flock, who are
risking their lives for Christ in the field of battle,
he would further animate them, "having ascer-
tained the heart of the Pope"; and recalling his
many brave priests abused, imprisoned, deported
as criminals, and who, like Fathers Batiz and
Lopez, gave their lives for their flock, he glori-
fies God for giving him sons "who will not suc-
cumb before the persecutors nor abdicate the
dignity of Christians and of men."

Rome Sanctions Fight for Liberty

He is still more consoled to hear "the words of
Holy Eulogy, of benediction, and of special love
that you have merited from the Supreme Head

of the Church. . . . We have seen the Holy Father bless your heroic resistance, approve your acts, applaud your sacrifices. . . . In fact, the Supreme Pontiff encourages all of us, priests and faithful, to persevere resolutely in our attitude, scorning all threats; and he has addressed this special message to the youth of Mexico: 'Fear nothing and no one, except treason to your conscience.'"

Archbishop Gonzales sent further specific approval: "You have not provoked this armed movement. But having exhausted pacific means, the movement exists, and to our Catholic sons who have risen in arms in the defense of their social and religious rights, after having pondered deeply before God and having consulted the most learned theologians in the City of Rome, we say to them: Be tranquil in your conscience and receive our blessing. . . . Do not be faint-hearted for a moment. Christ, the King, Eternal Victor, is with you. For Him we struggle, for Him we risk our lives, for Him we shall not permit that Mexico be deprived of infinite good; for Him we shall continue resisting the iniquitous assaults, until Mexico be guaranteed, by means of justice and charity, an era of true Christian liberty . . ."

This unequivocal sanction strengthened the Primate's uncompromising attitude to the religion-killing laws and their enforcers; and it nerved the Cristeros to more strenuous battle for "God, Faith, Fatherland." But they were soon confronted with more crushing opposition than the cohorts of Calles and the United States embargoes. On April 22, 1928, they lost in the death of Archbishop Mora, the exiled Primate of Mexico, their strongest defender of armed defense;

and the Mexican episcopate lost a leader not easily replaced. Some extracts from Archbishop Drossaerts' pronouncement at his obsequies in San Antonio, clarify the crucial conditions of that time, and at this hour are even more relevant:

"Liberty is being crucified at our door and the United States contemplates the tragedy with indifference. . . . Has despotism become popular among us? Are we not trying to gain the friendship and favor of the men whose hands are bathed in the blood of uncountable victims, while poor Mexico lies wounded to death, bound hand and foot with the chains that we have helped to forge? Did we not support Carranza and the arch-bandit Villa and raise Obregon to the presidency? Have we not sent Calles the airplanes with which he is now bombarding the heroic men who are dying for liberty of conscience in Jalisco? We ourselves are, in great measure, responsible for this Mexican tragedy."

Noting that such was the poverty of the Mexican Church that her exiled priests and prelates had not enough to pay for their own funerals, and that they had sought no armed intervention, the Archbishop added words vibrant today:

"No, we want no war with Mexico. But surely decency, humanity and love of liberty demand a virile protest from civilized nations, and first of all from this nation of the Monroe Doctrine, against the brutal and barbarous policy of a government that tramples on all liberties. The voice of the United States has made itself heard in Armenia, in Cuba, in Russia.

"Why, then, this ominous silence of our State Department, of our Congress, of our press, of our pulpit? Have we forgotten that this Republic was founded by men who held that resistance to tyranny is obedience to God?"

U. S. Silence on Calles Atrocities

Today, seven years later, Archbishop Drossaerts has had to raise indignant voice in behalf of a greater number of Mexican Prelates exiled in San Antonio, including Most Rev. Leopoldo Ruiz y Flores, Apostolic Delegate to Mexico. His declaration at the obsequies of the noble exiled Primate of Mexico, that "liberty is crucified at our door, and the United States contemplates the tragedy with indifference," unhappily remained true thereafter. This ringing appeal of the Prelate who had most intimate knowledge of the tyrannous atrocities and whose heart bled and still bleeds for their victims, fell echoless on press, people, and government.

Although the horrors perpetrated by Calles' hirelings on the Catholic population, and the feats of the Gorostieta forces in defense and reprisal, supplied news material that should capture any literary market, these items were quarantined more effectively by our press than were pest ships in our ports. Catholic weeklies broke but rarely the sudden silence that brought the Columbian campaign to anti-climax; and the secular organs grew absolutely dumb, except when echoing the Calles publicity, that beyond the Rio Grande all was quiet as once on the Potomac.

Even McCullagh's Revealing Picture Barred

Yet the most famous of international reporters was then in Mexico gathering news as startling

as that with which he had been the first to shock
the world from Russia and the Orient. One great
New York daily was eager to publish this fin-
ished journalist's script, deeming it the "scoop"
of the year; but the millionaire owner forbade
the editor to touch it. And all our other monster
dailies, that spend fortunes for such findings in
lands afar, yielded to like influences.

No publisher could be found in the United
States for this masterly first-hand record of the
shocking atrocities on our border at that hour;
and Francis McCullagh, the most noted of world
correspondents, had to go to London to find a
publisher for his authentic account of the events
in "Red Mexico." It remains the most graphic
and enlightening exposition the subject has elicited, and is as timely now as in 1928.

"Red Mexico" paints the men and the motives
and their revealing background, the plots, murders, massacres, and counterblasts, the Mexico-
Washington interactions, and the contrast of
rulers and people, in true and vivid colors.

Changing names and dates, this 1927 picture
would be equally descriptive of the present
scenes, except that 1935 is more ruinously "Red."

Mr. McCullagh holds up compellingly to the
seeing eye the outrages and heroisms and international treasons and trickeries that the present
narrative can merely outline. Yet the last seven
years can double or treble the record he presents
for the previous fourteen (1914-1928), of some
twelve hundred murders, twenty-five hundred
property seizures, a thousand robberies and kid-
nappings, two hundred expulsions, and about
seven thousand arrests. In fact the grounds for

his every charge and appeal to the American conscience are more peremptory now.

Parleying With An Irresponsible Tyranny

The appeal was strong enough then to excite informed consciences to action; but just as "Red Mexico" appeared in 1928, packed with compelling arguments, the policy of combat was reversed. With Archbishop Mora's death, his strong policy of absolute resistance to resolute oppressors of religion was in eclipse; and some American advisors induced his exiled successor, Archbishop Ruiz, to accept their mediation with Calles. Deeming themselves assured of the helpful influence of our government and the good offices of Ambassador Morrow, they apparently assumed that United States persuasions in peaceful negotiation would suddenly change the leopard's spots, transmuting Red into White.

Negotiations were opened by the Rev. John J. Burke, C. S. P., who, according to "The Church in Mexico" pamphlet of his National Catholic Welfare Conference, had no official warrant from the United States administration, but merely the informal statement of President Coolidge's pleasure, could Mr. Morrow, "also informally," arrange a conference between the Mexican government and the Catholic authorities.

Father Burke held conferences with Calles April 4, 1928, and a second, accompanied by Archbishop Ruiz, on May 17, when an agreement was reached. But this was not ratified until more than a year later, June 4, 1929, when it was signed and published by President Portes Gil, and by Archbishop Ruiz and Bishop Diaz.

Prefacing that he will apply the Constitution of the Republic and the laws derived therefrom, without favor, the Mexican president merely guaranteed: 1. The law requiring the registration of ministers applies only to those approved by their hierarchical superior. 2. The laws prohibiting all religious instruction in all schools whether private or public do not prevent it within the confines of the church. 3. The right of petition guaranteed by the laws to all citizens applies also to the members of any church. In recognizing "the identity" of the Church, he deliberately excludes, as does his constitution, the Church's legal personality, which was at the root of all grievances.

A "Settlement" That Proved Unsettling

On the strength of the good will implied in these concessions, if concessions they be, Archbishop Ruiz announced, as Apostolic Delegate, that "the Mexican clergy will resume religious services pursuant to the laws in force." Churches were reopened, but "in accordance with the number of priests allowed by the different state governments." There was further agreement that the Bishops would call off the Cristero insurrection, and the government would grant complete amnesty to all the insurrectionists.

The settlement met with general distrust and gravely alarmed the League of Liberty Leaders and their most eminent supporters, lay and cleric. Becoming cognizant of its contents, as adopted at the secret conference of May, 1928, they protested vigorously to Rome, on grounds which, they claim, averted papal sanction at that time.

They further allege that personal assurances had later been transmitted to Rome that the Hoover administration would guarantee the compact and offer ambassadorial services to enlarge and extend it; and that in view of such hope the Holy Father's previous rejection was withdrawn.

Church Left Defenseless to Faithless Tyrants

The outstanding leaders insisted that submission to the government registration of priests and limitation of their numbers, and to the exclusion of religious teaching from even their own schools, would put them in a worse position than before; and the suppression of the armed Cristero movement would leave the Catholics defenseless against the absolute and unhindered power that this agreement was conferring on the persecutors.

No trust could be put in the alleged security for future betterment unless they themselves retained the physical power to exact it; for they were convinced that Mr. Morrow would stand with the Calles gang as he had consistently been doing, and there was no hope of United States support. The promised amnesty would be but a sentence of death to the Cristero leaders, for the pledges of the Calles faction were worthless; and thus the Church they were defending, in leaving them helpless, would be doing for Calles what he and his armies had been unable to effect.

In opposing all treaties with faithless and unprincipled persecutors they were able to cite one of the negotiators in support. Bishop Diaz had made several such pronouncements in the United States; and in his final statement to the American people as executive secretary of the Mexican

Hierarchy, April 7, 1927, he covers admirably the present situation. He declared it absolutely futile for the United States or the Catholic Church to negotiate disputes with the Calles government, since their word and their laws, which are equally changeable, afford no basis of trust.

Compromise "Bears Germ of Corruption"

"No settlement is possible between any right thinking people and an irresponsible tyranny. The government of Mexico," he said, "is a ruthless bloodstained tyranny against which thousands of its people are in arms; and its Constitution, which was never submitted to the people, is an instrument fashioned by a selfish oligarchy for the robbery of United States nationals as of their own." It can authorize any theft or tyrrany; hence there could be no settlement until that doctrine of persecution and thievery is repudiated.

Eager to carry on its spiritual ministrations, the Church had relied on this and that politician's promises that their laws against it would not be enforced; but now bitter experience has shown that compromise is no longer possible. "The Church led no armed rebellion; but it was good Catholic doctrine as it was good American doctrine, that forcible resistance to an unjust tyranny is the righteous duty of a citizen; and he was proud to say that his people in Mexico are true to the right and are justifying their faith by the blood of martyrs."

Archbishop Ruiz's recent pastoral shows that they have returned to this position, based on the principle of Bishop Diaz's final word in 1927·

"Eventually right will triumph in Mexico as it always triumphs. IT WILL NOT TRIUMPH THROUGH A COMPROMISE THAT IN ITS VERY NATURE BEARS THE GERM OF CORRUPTION."

Gorostieta and Cristeros Protest

This was precisely the view of the Cristero leaders whose hold on the great central states was firmest in 1929. Their unconquered forces were then presenting a serious menace to Callism; and they deemed the negotiations a Calles trick to escape it. General Gorostieta sent to Archbishop Ruiz, May 16, 1929, a vigorous protest that reports of parleying with Callism were bringing to the men under arms a chill of death far worse than the perils they had faced. It was but the device of a government dripping with blood to get their National Guard of twenty thousand effectives to surrender the arms they had wrested from that government, which had flouted two million signatures and consented to negotiate only when confronted with arms. Once the arms are laid down they will again flout Episcopate and people. It is the National Guard that must solve the problem, which is not solely a religious one but embraces all liberties. The National Guard alone watches over all the interests of the people from whom it has sprung, and its arms are their only guarantee of justice.

Could the Bishops, Gorostieta added, have remained with their people and given them undivided support in this obligatory battle for their liberties the tyrants' power would have long ago been shattered. Nevertheless, the national army,

poor in armament but rich in military virtue, is
fighting with greater success each day, determined to recover all the liberties of their people,
and they have fixed as their objective not the
empty promises of treacherous tyrants but un-
conditional capitulation:

"Material resources we can ourselves obtain.
We ask the Episcopate to furnish the moral force
that will make us invincible, by counseling a
virile, united attitude proper of Christians, not of
slaves. Are we not bound together by the blood
of two hundred martyred priests and thousands
of other martyrs?"

As representing an important section of the
great Institution they govern, Gorostieta requested the Bishops to present this petition to the
Holy Father in the hope of terminating the prev-
alent confusion and empowering the National
Guard to win its fight for God, Fatherland, and
Liberty.

Gorostieta Leadership Survives Untimely Death

It was a prophetic document, and the Mexican
Episcopate as well as people are now giving
united response to its appeal. But before the par-
leys ended the brave commander-in-chief was
shot in ambuscade and he died pressing the crucifix to his heart. Learning of this disaster, a
ship bearing him ample munitions returned to
the United States; and both events facilitated the
surrender prescribed in the "Adjustment," of
which the people got their first intimation from
the press June 22, 1929.

Despite the general disapproval of the terms,
and their actual ineffectiveness, the Apostolic

Delegate and Bishop Diaz, who was named Arch-bishop of Mexico City on the signing of the com-pact, were motivated by weighty considerations. The closing of all churches had proved a dan-gerous defense; for the consequent lack of re-ligious services and priestly direction, together with the disorders inseparable from revolution-ary action, was gravely imperiling religion; and it was felt that at all costs worship should be re-stored. More trust was placed in informal assurances of the American administration and its informal representatives than a more intimate knowledge of Mr. Morrow and his connections with Calles would have warranted.

Besides, the Catholics in the United States had grown silent on Mexican grievances. No protests nor petitions from their own brethren abroad nor from any other quarter were pressing the Ameri-can administration to take action against perse-cution or persecutors, and there was no likeli-hood of its lifting the embargoes that crippled the Cristeros. It was a choice between two evils, and they took the way of peace.

All Pledges Broken When Defenders Disband

No peace resulted. Within a week President Portes Gil declared at a Masonic banquet that he would see to it that the Constitution and laws were entirely and strictly enforced; and that as a Mason and as President he had yielded nothing. This was in fact true of the substance of the com-pact; but now he had publicly repudiated in word the good will he had expressed in it; and he and his fellows began at once to repudiate in deeds the amnesty he had definitely pledged.

Within a month five hundred surrendered Cristeros were shot, or murdered in their homes, their property seized, and their persecuted families left destitute; and altogether five thousand Cristeros and hundreds of priests shared the same fate. This, with the expulsion of Episcopate and clergy and all sisterhoods, leaving but some two hundred registered priests—most of them fingerprinted like criminals — for over fifteen million people, and the stamping of the Moscow brand of atheizing communism on every school and office in the land, are now blazoning to the world the cost of compromise with irresponsible tyranny; and, therewith the lesson, that no compact of liberty is possible unless tyranny shall first be uprooted.

"Germ of Corruption" and Destruction

Bishop Diaz' statement that no compromise with Mexico's tyranny is possible and the only way to mend it is to end it, proved true in the very year of the one-sided concordat, which precluded the Church's legal personality and permitted the state to prescribe the number of her ministers.

As the Pope's encyclical stated, it had nothing but its promise of "good will" to recommend it; and this good will was at once disavowed by Congress and Party and the President who pledged it, and by the vigorous renewal of countless acts of varied and universal persecution.

The armistice was broken by the slaughter of every Cristero fighter or suspect that could be reached; and the assaults that followed on priests, sisters, churches, schools, and Christian people were worse and more numerous than

McCullagh's "Red Mexico" records for the previous decade. The country became more and more reddened with murdered blood as the Calles procedure took on the fullness of Moscow Red. I have a list of hundreds of outrages on churches and clergy and people, without a single instance of punishment for the perpetrators. These are news items culled from the daily papers, with date and place; and though they are but a fraction of the atrocities recorded, they cover some fifty pages.

Churches and shrines seized, desecrated, burned, or bombed; priests assaulted even during church services, injured, murdered, or expelled; states limiting the number of priests to one for fifty thousand or one hundred thousand people, or totally excluding them as in Tabasco since 1925 and in fifteen states at this writing; the accompanying sacrileges and outrages on person and property with the ever-increasing prevalence of de-religionizing and demoralizing teachings in the schools after the Canabal fashion in Tabasco, and the expulsion of the protesting Apostolic Delegate and nearly all the Episcopate, prove that the pledge of "good will' was but a trick.

Removing all armed opposition, this treacherous treaty left the Calles forces free to accomplish unrestricted the determined communist purpose to tear out religion, root and branch, from the hearts and homes as well as the schools and temples of Mexico.

How Cardenas-Canabal Masons Eradicate God

This purpose, as authoritatively stated within a week of the good will compact and many times since, is well expressed in the letter of Convocation to the Masonic Anti-clerical Convention at Guadalajara, July 20, 1933, at which the present President Cardenas presided: "God is a myth; religion is a fable; the clergy are bureaucrats of the theological farce"; and on this basis they would operate "for the Emancipation of Human Thought."

Their most perfect emancipator, then and now, was the recent dominating member of the cabinet, Garrido Canabal, whose naked exemplifications of emancipating minds from morality were extended to all schools by Secretary of Education Bassols, also recent cabinet minister, and are now constitutionally authorized.

Canabal had other emancipating methods which were also copied widely. Their officials, like themselves, practice with immunity the immoralities they preach, and brothels are an official industry. Such sources swell the millionaire wealth of ex-President Rodriguez in Lower California and of Canabal in Tabasco, and they uphold their agents in like emancipatory methods.

Canabal had 85 villagers of Paraiso hanged in a body because some of them had lynched a municipal agent who had ravished and mortally wounded a girl of fourteen; and he sent his Red Shirts to execute some hundred others who were fleeing to another state for Christian security.

It is significant that two hundred of his Red Shirts proceeded recently on a similar mission to Jalisco; but none of them returned. Countless such instances of incredible barbarity illustrate the emancipating or "defanaticizing" methods which followed the 1929 covenant, and to which the recent government had given its highest sanction by raising the chief Exemplifiers, Canabal, Rodolfo Calles and Bassols, to cabinet rank.

Penalizing God, Even on Children's Lips

The Apostolic Delegate and Archbishop Diaz have recently reaffirmed that the conditions and accompaniments of persecution are immeasurably worse than in 1926, which is also evidenced in the atrocities recorded in the Mexican dailies, though these are heavily hampered by government censorship. The murderous assaults on worshippers at Coyoacan and Tacubaya and Santa Catalina, and the seizure and imprisonment of priests in the Federal District happen to reach us because witnessed by foreign reporters at the capital. But the government has taken measures to prevent such mistakes in the future, and hundreds of infamies throughout the nation wrought by Canabal's now official Red Shirts and other federal agents have not been permitted to leak out. Many of these are connected with the atheizing and sex teaching educational program, which has resulted in the almost universal boycotting of the state schools.

Police and soldiers have been sent out to seek the children on the streets and in the homes and force them into empty classrooms. The consequent outrages on resisting mothers and weeping children are numerously recorded under "Leva de Ninos" (seizure of children) in the Mexican dailies; also such items as the savage beatings of children at Naco, Sonora, who objected to atheistic teachings and, bidden to repeat: "No hay Dios" (There is no God) cried out, "Hay Dios, hay Dios."

Defenders Arm, and Students Tell Mr. Hull

"The Fathers of Families" and other parents' organizations have been forming a network of home classes, graded from house to house, and the violent outrages to which these were especially subjected have stimulated the wide resumption of armed defense as in the days of the Cristeros. The accepted name is now Libertadores, defenders of all liberties.

La Prensa has been reporting since early 1935 the repulse of the Red Shirts and other official atheistic enforcers in various states, and the wide increase of rebellious groups throughout the country. Reports accumulate of the organized protests of university students against the government's socialistic monopoly of education and its communistic teachings, and the general sensation created by a manifesto of the University Students' Federation to the President.

Attributing the evils of Mexico to a government subversive of natural rights and salutary customs, they demand that Cardenas expel from his cabinet such "communist" proprietors of the best ranches and largest industries as Telles and Canabal, and also that he forbid Mr. Daniels, the garrulous foreign eulogist of their perverse rule, to intervene in Mexico's domestic affairs.

This, by the way, is a pertinent reply to Secretary Hull's contention that the Higgins and Borah resolutions would involve us in Mexico's internal affairs; whereas, on the contrary, they coincide with the urgings of Mexico's most cultured representatives, that we stop the intervention we are making and silence or recall an intervening blunderer.

Such items as these were soon made difficult to glean. The resolutions in the United States Congress and the universal protest they connote had so alarmed the Mexican Junta that they even out-Moscowed Moscow in the arbitrary extension of dictatorial power.

Bars All Writings Not Canabal Cultured

Their nominal mouthpiece, President Cardenas, issued a decree, February 13, in virtue of the extraordinary powers conferred on him by Congress, that, since it is an ideological tendency of the government to combat fanaticism and religious prejudice with a firm resolve to effect the spiritual liberation of the people: Therefore, in order to prevent registration or circulation of publications and printed matter and correspondence that imply diffusion of any creed or ideas contrary to the culture of the National Revolutionary Party, it is hereby decreed that all registration and circulation is prohibited of any correspondence or writings offensive to the National Government or diffusive of any religious doctrine whatsoever.

This extraordinary decree expresses well the Mexican tyranny's de-civilized if not demonized "ideology." It opens to their spies all personal correspondence as well as prints, native and foreign, and shuts them out or suppresses them at pleasure, thus tearing down the safeguards of all privacy and the free press pillar of democracy. And whereas the United States, like all civilized governments, excludes only obscene and demoralizing matter from the mails, the Mexican government throws them open to all that is debasing and unclean, and shuts them against what normal nations deem most purifying and ennobling.

It might puzzle even Ambassador Daniels how to include such procedures in his blanket eulogies of Mexico's government; and it should strain Secretary Hull's interpretation of "internal affairs," even if their seizure of the valuable American-owned lands of Las Rusias has not moved him to revise it.

Juarez Outrage on Women and Church

An outrage of more common occurrence, that has excited attention because perpetrated on the American border before the eyes of our citizens, occurred recently at Juarez within sight of El Paso on the Rio Grande. There is at Juarez the ancient and venerated Church of Our Lady of Guadalupe, and though all priests were expelled from the state, Father Salvador Uranga remained at this shrine protected by devoted people. He was forcibly deported February 7, and a notorious government agent named Elorduy was sent to take possession of the church.

When over a hundred matrons who had assembled at the shrine protested against the intrusion, Elorduy, after the example of Canabal's Red Shirts in the Federal District, fired upon the ladies until his revolver was empty, and then beat them with the butt. Five were dangerously wounded, and there is no doubt of his acquittal or pardon by the Federal authorities.

Witnessing Bishop Sees But One Solution

In fact, it was but one of hundreds or even thousands of more flagrant atrocities, and it was only its proximity to El Paso that furnished it publicity. The Most Reverend Anthony Schuler, S. J., Bishop of El Paso, made it the subject of some comment that deserves serious consideration from press and President and Congress.

Living in sight of Mexico and in daily touch for years with its exiled priests and sisterhoods and people, to whom he has given hospitable refuge, Bishop Schuler knows better the antagonistic relations of rulers and people and the causes and destructive effects of persecution than perhaps any other American; and he is thus qualified by wide experience to determine the best solution for the restoration of peace and civilized order.

The Juarez incident, he said, was but an instance of countless occurrences of like anti-religious nature, often more abhorrent and injurious, that are perpetrated daily throughout the length and breadth of Mexico; and they are bound to continue and grow worse so long as the laws that authorize them and the rulers that instigate and enforce them are sustained by United States recognition and the compelling support which our government permits it to include.

Withdrawal of U. S. Recognition Ends Tyranny

Besides having the effect of securing recognition from foreign governments and excluding these from vindication of their rights, our recognition has been permitted to include extraordinary loaning facilities and free access to arms and munitions even from government arsenals, while we exercise the utmost vigilance in barring all such sources from Mexico's forces of liberty.

It is this that keeps the Mexicans crushed in

fact under the heels of an armed minority and crushed in spirit by denial of hope. Let our government, said Bishop Schuler, withdraw recognition from the government of Mexico or manifest its dissatisfaction with the rabid persecution of civil and religious liberty, and soon the Mexican people would settle the question to their own satisfaction and to ours, in the establishment of an orderly, civilized, and democratic government.

It is a simple solution and it is the only one. Referring to our intervention, a Mexican patriot recently wrote, "We feel as if a mighty hand is crushing us all." Let us but withdraw that hand from the party of tyranny, and even though we do not extend it to the party of liberty, they will themselves be able to vindicate their freedom.

CHAPTER X

GOOD NEIGHBORS TO CRUCIFIERS AND CORRUPTERS

THE friendly visitor who enters the offices and homes of Mexico and notes its family life cannot fail to realize that the Mexicans are, as a whole, a kindly, Christian, liberty-loving people. This would be gathered from their history, though not as Americans usually have written it; and personal acquaintance will discover in the highest and the lowliest patient fortitude and sterling virility clothed in a generous kindliness and a courtesy of manners that bespeak the essence of Christian culture.

Our account of the heroic struggle of Gorostieta's Libertadores, while our government was tying their fighting hands and arming their tyrants, exposes the flippant ignorance of such comments as a correspondent contributed to the **Commonweal**; that either the Mexican majority are a helpless lot or there is something wrong with their clergy; and of the more shallow editorial comment that our line should be, "not to weaken the Mexican government, but to strengthen the Mexican Church." '

If they are helpless, it is because we, as a nation, Catholics included, have kept them so by furnishing all our help to their oppressors; and to talk of not weakening a government that has

professedly set itself by law and force to uproot
religion and all accepted social standards is but a
plea for support of the Soviet system.

Glorious Record of Mexican Clergy

The gibes at the Mexican clergy and Church,
which have wider circulation, are equally mis-
placed. Considering the long years of ruthless re-
pression that have been outlined, the closing and
confiscation of seminaries and the exclusion of
Christian teaching, the expulsion of religious
orders, the encouragement of faithlessness and
the penalizing of loyalty, it is a thrilling surprise
to find that the surviving Mexican clergy, secular
and regular, have come through it all practically unscathed; and often with a record of heroism that few of their contemporaries can match.

There are few records of persecution that can
present less than one per cent of clerical defec-
tions when high rewards were offered for apos-
tasy; yet not a dozen out of more than four thousand priests in Mexico can be so recorded. Priests
are legally expelled from more than half the dioceses and little more than two hundred are tolerated in the remainder; but some two thousand
are still there bravely working for their people in
penury and hardship at the risk of liberty and
life. Arrest and imprisonment of priests is an
almost daily newspaper item, and the legal penalty for saying Mass or for any religious minis-
tration is five hundred pesos and thirty days
imprisonment, subject to indefinite extension.

I met in Mexico City a visting physician from
a state where for ten years no priest was permitted to register and the de-religionizing campaign

was notorious for its irrational and violent extremes, including the prohibition of all sacred names and symbols for any usage whatsoever. He had a Sacred Heart medallion on his lapel, and a crucifix was interwoven in his finger ring; and to the remark that he could not wear these in that state, the doctor replied: "I do wear them and I defy that Governor to touch them. There are hundreds whom I have served for thirty years, including his own officials, who warn or guard me against his plots on my life. He has decreed the expulsion of our priests, but priests are there working among their people; and I am today taking fresh ammunition to the men we have armed in the hills to protect them, or if need be, to avenge them."

Hunted Priests and Prelates Guarded by Flock

Numerous priests, also toiling in disguise among their people, assured me that men of such calibre assist and make their labors possible. There are hunted Bishops, too, who have managed to cling to their dioceses through all the persecutions, and some who were deported have returned in various guise, often to pontificate in rags. Archbishop Orozco, worn with seventy years' toil, is again traversing the mountain ranges guarded by his brave Jaliscans.

In another set of mountain ranges there is a Bishop whose name may not now be told, for federal assassins are upon his track, but it will loom large in history. A theologian of highest rank, a scholar, an orator, a teacher and writer of distinction, this prelate has for nine years defied decrees of expulsion and, despite constant espionage, has traversed the Sierra Madre from crag to crag, bringing encouragement to his people, who in turn risk their lives in his defense.

The Mexican Constitution also prohibits priestly training. This Bishop is providing for the priesthood of the future. There is a rude log cabin in the Sierra Madre which is dormitory, dining room, lecture and study hall and chapel for twenty-two young men whom he himself is training for the ministry and providing the complete ecclesiastical course. Often flying for their lives, they build another log seminary in a more remote Sierra fastness. In the Irish penal days Bishop O'Gallagher held such a seminary in the mountains of Donegal, and, driven thence, he trained other youths in mud-walled huts in the Bog of Allen. From that school came several patriot prelates, among them Dr. Doyle, of Kildare and Leighlin, who divides with O'Connell the honors of Catholic emancipation. May we not expect that emancipators of faith and country will yet issue from that log seminary of the Sierra, where again Bishop and priest aspirants meet "feloniously to learn?"

Mexican Officials Refurbish Historic Lies

Yet Cardenas and the other Calles claquers proclaim, with their wonted mendacious hypocrisy, that there is no persecution of religion. They are merely executing the laws; and so was Henry VIII when the "contumacy" of Cardinal Fisher and Sir Thomas More lost them their heads. But they have gone immeasurably further in persecuting virulence than even the worst of Henry's British successors or Roman predecessors. Their laws, as we have abundantly shown, are aimed and framed for the utter extermination of religion; and they are executed with a ruthless thoroughness that history could not parallel till Lenin founded and Stalin perfected an organism for dethroning God. And not merely in the temples of worship. Only some two hundred churches in Mexico are tolerated now; and the ruling bloc had posted motions for the confiscation of these also and for the clergy's total expulsion. This is but the initial step. When proposing the atheizing amendment, Senator Padilla said religion has always survived persecution, and it cannot be extinguished by destroying churches and expelling or killing off its clergy.

Moulding a Communist Generation

Religion is in the heart and mind, and will never die until rooted out of them. The law had already excluded religion from all teachings; now they must utilize all teachings to eradicate religion from all hearts, infusing instead the soul of the revolution, and thus create a genuine Communist generation. This the amendment is framed to accomplish as adequately as ingenuity of words can phrase it; and the Cardenas decree of rigid enforcement for this de-religionizing program in all the schools of Mexico proclaims a persecution of religion more absolute and venomous than Julian the Apostate had devised.

The nation-wide student revolt forced the government to exclude its application to universities; and now there is a revolt within the universities because the government is supplanting the professors with incompetent Communist creatures.

In addition to numerous public protests, the national manifesto of the University Students' Federation condemned the official socialism imposed on them as the demagogic pretext of a reactionary monopolistic government, to whose members it has brought luxury and wealth, but to the people only misery and hunger through strikes, robbery, and blood-stained persecution. They demanded expulsion of such millionaire Cabinet Communists as Canabal; but his Red Shirts and other organized supporters countered by congratulating the government on its courageous efficiency in infusing the soul of Soviet Communism into the schools and all the social and industrial activities of the nation.

To this Soviet soul the bloc of revolutionary youth is giving further nurture under government patronage. Members of the bloc sing the marching tune imposed on the children of the schools, "Uno, dos: No hay Dios" (One, two: there is no God); and they are everywhere distributing handbills that tell child and youth to despise and hate their own fathers who forbid them the schools of the revolution and hold them in slavery to religion's "fanatic" bonds: "Break the bestial yoke of him you call father and of her you call mother and run to the schools of the revolution, where socialist masters will teach you to be free." The full version of this document as published in the press, should show our State Department that the Soviet it recognized afar is now rampant on our borders.

None But Atheists Need Apply

The papers report that Canabal, when dominant

force in the Cabinet, had a thousand of these organized ruffians under a system of atheistic training; and he and his fellows saw to it that their demoniac fury against religion got practical enforcement. Every department has sent out a questionnaire to all teachers and directors, officials and employes, in schools, banks, public utilities, and in all industries and social organizations of every description, demanding that said employes or applicants shall state whether they profess, practice, or propagate the principles of the Revolution; whether they ever attended church or Mass or any other religious service, or permit their wives or children to do so; whether they ever took part in religious processions, or had relatives who were priests or were enemies of the Revolution. There is a long list of similar soul-searching in order to have absolute surety that none but a simon-pure anti-religious Communist shall have place or office in Mexico, and that wherever, directly or indirectly, the government's power can reach, all shall be excluded from position and economic employment who are even suspected of belief in God.

These questionnaires are public documents. Article 3 of the Constitution and its de-religionizing amendment, and the President's decree of rigorous enforcement, are public documents. Hence, if all other evidence of rabid and active persecution, not merely of the Catholic Church, but of all religion, were ignored, our State Department cannot but be cognizant that anti-religious Communism of the deepest Soviet dye is the driving force in the government and Cabinet of Mexico. The recent Cardenas decree of univer-

sal censorship should further enlighten them.
And President Cardenas' first pronouncement to
his new Cabinet, emphasizing its continuance,
shows that his change of Ministers indicates no
change of heart.

Referring to this ukase, **La Prensa** asked February 19: "How can there be doubt of anti-religious spirit in a government that excludes from
the mails, as corrupting literature, any work
whatsoever that teaches a religious idea?" This
decree excludes the "Imitation of Christ," the
"City of God," the works of Dante, Aquinas and
Bossuet and the Old and New Testaments. In
fact, all these and whatsoever other books or
prints, however classical or venerated, that have
the slightest religious reference or tendency have
been already weeded out of the national library
by order of the Secretary of Education. Nor has
its recently announced revocation broken at all
the bars on religious documents or personal letters of religious or civil opponents. Recent advices and personal experience prove the system
to be still in full swing.

Our Postmaster Franks Calles Propaganda

The Cardenas decree was applied to all federal
libraries and could include the home. This may
happen; for nothing is incredible in Communist
Mexico, and it would be but an extension
of actual practice. I have been in homes, and
have evidence of countless others, where family
libraries have been robbed and mutilated by
government agents. A type of such institutional robbery may be seen at Topotzutlan, some
forty miles from the capital, where mutilated

books of many filchings are stacked along with the rare Jesuit library in the basement of that great collegiate institution, a monument of art and architecture which enlightened zeal and sacrifice had built and made the medium for centuries of civilizing culture. This is the "historic jewel," which the Masonic Lodges, August 20, 1935, forbade to be restored to the church!

Our Postoffice Department has meekly complied with the Cardenas requirements and promptly informed some of our most worthy American publications of their exclusion from Mexico, while admitting Mexico's scurrilous publicity post free. Shall we brook the humiliation of seeing our State Departments become the obedient servants of Mexican tyranny in suppressing the rights and liberties of press and people, which they are constituted to guard and are sworn to preserve?

The Cardenas decree was intended to preclude any prints or writings of religious or freedom-loving tint from reaching the schools on which he had imposed an atheist curriculum. To the promotion of this atheizing system he and his masters are bending their energies, with an openness of malignant methods that neither the United States Embassy nor State Department can ignore. In fact, the determination which Calles proclaimed July, 1934, and his congress has since embodied in the Constitution and the last presidential decree has clamped on the schools, that "The Revolution" must take possession of all consciences, has now so clearly revealed its subversiveness of human decencies and of human nature itself that the failure of our Ambas-

sador to retract his fulsome eulogies of scheme
and schemer deepens into a diplomatic mystery.

Mr. Daniels must have noted the widespread
publicity under government patronage of the
"Bloc of Revolutionary Youth," which was inciting the children of Mexico to hate their own
fathers and mothers who forbid them atheistic
schooling, and to burst the parental bonds that
hold them in "fanatic slavery."

Official Revolt Against Nature and Civilization

There is even more authoritative proof that
"The Revolution," which the Calles education
feeds and fosters, is an absolute revolt against nature as well as God. "The Tenth Proletarian Congress of the Red Syndicate," which was officially
sponsored by the Secretary of Education, lays
down among other "Postulates" of Socialistic
Education:

"Until today the child has been the victim of
his elders. The teachers, an exploited caste for
their own protection must join our movement to
destroy the parasitic classes such as the Catholics, the Protestants, the intellectuals, and the
bourgeoisie. These must be utterly destroyed.
The Mexican teachers, having no clear understanding nor strong unions, will try to pretend
and to deceive; our Red Syndicate will place
spies in the schools to see to it that the Socialist
education will be actually imparted. All children
over five years of age must belong to the State,
and not to the clergy nor to their parents.

"All the burdens that weigh upon humanity
were produced by the clergy, as the exploitation
of the farmers and laborers by means of the doc-

trine of Eternity. The Protestant ministers, the Catholic priests, the Bishops, and the Pope are dangerous reptiles. We must banish them all.

"No God exists. Religion is a theological myth. The bible is nothing but an enormous lie.

"Down with all professional men; down with the bourgeoisie; and down with the universities, the incubators of both.

"NO MORE IDOLS; NO MORE FATHERS OF FAMILIES; NO MORE RESPECT- ABLES; NO MORE BOSSES; NO MORE GOD."

This is no blatant raving of soap box ranters; it is the mind and method of the masters of Mexico. Propagated by the authorized organizations of the older and of the younger members of the National Revolutionary Party under the direction of the Secretary of Education, these "postulates" define the meaning and express precisely the purpose of what they call Revolution. It is a revolt against God and against all that is sacred in the traditions and decencies not only of Christian but of pagan civilization.

Children Drilled to Hate God and Parents

Nor is the systematic organization of adults and of adolescents, and of militant Red Shirts and "Revolutionary Youth" and other juvenile sections into rampant Red propagandists, deemed sufficient for this purpose. The very children must be drilled in organized revolt against God.

The Calles' command last July, promptly legalized and already in full operation, to capture the children's consciences and root out of them in the schools all faith in God and reverence for priest and parent, is now extended to the kindergarten and supplementary courses, in order to create more speedily "a new national soul" and beat the young as well as old into one national revolutionary pulp. An order from the Secretary of Education, endorsed and enforced the plan of the official head of the P. N. R. to organize the little children into P. N. R. units and train them from earliest childhood in the God-hating, priesthating communist postulates and preachments of their National Revolutionary Party.

It seems incredible, as Moscow was long incredible; but facts as the Mexican journals present them are horrifying beyond the reaches of fiction. It is Moscow in Mexico; but with a difference in favor of Moscow. Mexico calls it Socialism as that sounds softer to American ears; but in all its anti-religious teachings, and in all its economic theories, and in all its practices, except one, it is Marxian Communism as Lenin moulded it and as Stalin executes it with sanguinary efficiency.

Communist Chiefs Capitalist Grafters

This they proudly proclaim among themselves, and they boast of it in congress and senate, pointing definitely to Moscow for inspiration and example; but in one item of performance they have disappointed Moscow. They sent picked men to Russia to get intensified training in the Soviet system, and these returned qualified and eager to emulate if not better their masters. This they did very well, as far as Communism's de-religionizing content carried, in Tabasco and Sonora and other States whose governors had closer affinities to Calles.

Then Madam Kolontay came along as Ambassadress of Russia to exemplify Soviet Communism in person and extend its purest brand to all the States of Mexico. But this convinced and fanatic expoundress of Communism pure and undefiled soon experienced painful disillusion. The anti-religious basis of Communism was as sound in Mexico and its practice as perfect as Lenin or Stalin could desire, and the economic theory was also theirs; but the economic practice was quite otherwise.

Communism Caricatured Economically

It was Capitalism cornered by way of Communist cult. Peasant and peon were given the communist crumbs while the master communists took over for themselves the capitalistic dish. The Soviet minister's plain pronouncement hastened her withdrawal by request, as happened to Mr. Sheffield but not at all to Mr. Daniels; and still plainer speaking signalized her departure.

In her final message Madam Kolontay denounced Calles and his henchmen of the Revolutionary Party as false, hypocritical communists, who proclaimed that creed but utilized it for their own aggrandizement. They confiscated the best lands and estates and haciendas; but instead of distributing them among peons and people as their election trumpetings had pledged, they grabbed the rich properties and all that was valuable for themselves, leaving for their dupes what was sterile and worthless. As a result the governing cliques have utilized place and power to become capatalists, plutocrats, and millionaires, and the peasant poor are left poorer than before. What these self-serving hypocrites had enacted was but a caricaturing comedy of Communism.

From the economic standpoint the caricature has been taking louder coloring in the interim. Professor Halperin in "Current History," Mr. Marshall in the North American Alliance syndicate press, and other disinterested witnesses have shown that the wholesale appropriations of cultivated and productive properties have enriched the appropriating bosses, but their misuse of the best estates and their distribution of unfertile lands have wrought such general disorder and impoverishment that the vast body of the people would gladly see the National Revolutionary Party dumped into the Gulf.

General Insurrection Foreseen

This is why the numerous uprisings and local revolts, which appear in every issue of the Mexican dailies and seem to prelude a general insurrection, have no distinctive Church nor Catholic character; for they spring as much from civil and economic grievances as from religious persecution, perhaps even more.

The workers are dissatisfied with their wage which is far below the insufficient minimum the government had set; and **huelgas** or strikes, general and local, have been headline features in every daily for months. The peons and peasants, who have got unworkable allotments or none, are living in bitter disillusion, having not only failed to find the independent wealth assured them but lost their certainty of daily food.

Even the agrarian revolutionists are noisily protesting their discontent with their shares and the taxes and exactions that heavily discount them; and the official workers on government rolls, who form the majority of the working class, have realized that the government's requisition of some 5 percent of their less than living wage is no binding reward for party loyalty.

Still riper for revolt are the numerous school teachers and other state and federal employes, who have lost their positions for refusal to take the atheistic oath and swear to other minute anti-religious requirements, and the aggrieved officials who swallowed these oaths to keep their families from starving. The numerous and powerful university student bodies who are in open revolt against the government's imposition of incompetent teachers to propagate communist programs and who are demanding dismissal of the millionaire cabinet communists, will also welcome and forward any movement that shows promise of dislodging what they call "Callismo."

These and other grievances strengthen the general opposition on religious grounds. Though the Mexican people are over 90 percent Catholic and the anti-Calles elements have a larger Catholic percentage, not all are equally devoted to the Church by practice and profession. The successive confiscations of their churches and the banishment of their priests and the closing of Catholic seminaries and schools, with the absolute exclusion of religion from educational teachings and the moneyed ministrations of American sects, have necessarily diminished the knowledge and practice of religion. Yet these causes have had surprisingly little effect oñ the Faith itself.

Revolt On National Grounds, Religion Included

The marvel is that, despite such seemingly im-

possible handicaps, the essentials of religious
principles and precepts are held and treasured
widely. Over 2,000 "felon" priests still hide
among their people; and everywhere there is
evidence of devoted attachment to Christ the
King and His Virgin Mother. Even the Yaqui
and other tribes who, after their missions were
suppressed and their missionaries banished, frequently lapsed into paganism, retain their reverence for the Padres and Our Lady of Guadalupe.
In view of their fighting qualities the government
cultivates them by special appropriations; but
their banished Bishop visits them, and several
Jesuit missionaries also brave the government's
interdict. One of these who had been seven times
imprisoned, four times shot and wounded, and
twice sentenced to death, told me that the majority were more loyal to the Faith than to the
"Revolution," which gave them food and guns,
but robbed them of their Christian Fathers.*

But whether White, Mestizo, or Indian, Mexicans everywhere bear it ill that their shrines have
been desecrated and their most sacred traditions
reviled; and the government's concentrated campaign against God and Christ and religion and
all they held holy have alarmed a large number
that were hitherto indifferent. Hence, defense of
religion enters in a greater or less degree into
the motives of the various parties and interests
that are now organizing to overthrow their communist rulers. They are Catholics, and the more
dominant party is that which is more strongly
motived by the perils to their Faith; but they are

*This is Rev. Francisco Pichardo, S. J., who, returning to his Tara-
humaros, was imprisoned July 13 in Chihuahua and sentenced to
execution.

Mexicans all and equally intent on recovering their civic and economic liberty from the gang of tyrants that oppress them and the atheistic Communism that threatens to engulf them.

Atheist Peril Unifies Parties Of Discontent

It is the immediacy which this peril is presenting in the atheo-communist education that is unifying most widely and effectively all the parties of discontent. The Mexicans love their children, and Mexican mothers especially take their religion warmly to heart. Even indifferent fathers bitterly resent the atheistic educational system that would rob their children of all faith and reverence and uproot religion from their hearts. They see that if this conscience-killing school campaign is permitted to continue, their children and their children's children will be robbed of all their fathers revered and of all that charactered their people, and in a few generations the Mexico they love will be no more.

The educational amendment, in making unmistakably clear the government's settled purpose to atheize the nation, has had the good effect of solidifying in national unity the various parties that conflicting interests and delusive inducements had hitherto divided. Hence, the movement now under way is a struggle of 90 percent of the Mexican people for liberty; and not merely for Catholic liberties, but for all. It is not instigated nor dominated by the authorities of the Church, who have forbidden any armed movement or party of Catholics as such.

A misunderstanding of this position had created much discontent and division among the Catholic laity who, when assaulted and plunder-

ed by government satellites, resented what seemed their Church's prohibition to defend their
persons and properties by arms, the only method
available when all legal recourse was denied.

Laity Left Free To Determine Defense

These misconceptions have been cleared, and
Archbishop Ruiz, the Apostolic Delegate, has
stated definitely in his recent pastoral, that
whereas the Church does not permit armed defense of herself or of religion in her name, she
maintains firmly the right of a people to defend
themselves against tyranny and to vindicate their
natural liberties by arms when redress by legal
and peaceful means has proved impossible. This
the Mexican people have themselves to determine
and, should they resolve on armed defense, the
Church will have nothing to say, "neither promoting nor prohibiting."

This spreading insurgence is, then, a national
movement to liberate Mexico from the most destructive and corrupting despotism that ever got
foothold in this hemisphere, and to establish in
its stead a constitution and government that
guarantees civil and religious liberty for all.
They are seeking for Mexico essentially the same
liberty which Charles Carroll had in view in supporting American Independence, and which
American Catholics, whose services in winning
it Washington so signally commended, share
with their fellow citizens by constitutional right.

All priests and prelates, who are filched of
their citizenship by law, and all loyal Catholics
who are denied it by legal practice, want alike
to establish themselves as free citizens in a free

state. It is as much a struggle for liberty as was the American Revolution, except that the inciting tyranny is immeasurably more grievous; and they have more claim on our aid in securing it than had we on the people of France.

Interposal For Right Overdue

The parrot cry that this would be unwarranted interference in another country's "internal affairs" becomes, in the light of history, a laughing-stock. Congressman Celler's list of such "interferences" in the past, by the Department of State and by our Presidents in behalf of the oppressed, ranges through a century of time and over such distant lands as Russia, Turkey, Armenia, Morocco, Rumania, Esthonia, the Caucasus, Austria-Hungary, Germany, Switzerland, Hawaii, and Brazil. They rested on the principle expressed by Daniel Webster in the United States Senate in 1823, that it is perfectly proper for this country of free institutions and free exercise of natural rights to protest to any country in the world against persecution and oppression, of its own, or of other citizens.

Oppressive discrimination on religious grounds was in nearly all instances the occasion for our numerous and insistent interferences in the "internal affairs" of many nations. There is one instance of such interference in Mexico, that Mr. Lansing, when Secretary of State under President Wilson, made our recognition of the then **de facto** Mexican government conditional on their grant of freedom of worship to all the Mexican people, and that the then Mexican government accepted this condition without reservation.

The denial of such an agreement by the present Mexican Secretary of State has no more value than the denial by Cardenas of religious persecution at the very time he was issuing a decree forcing atheizing teaching on all the schools of Mexico. The outstanding fact, however, is, that while we were protesting freely against lesser and partial persecutions in distant lands, and against Mexican policies and deeds detrimental to our corporate and financial interests, neither the Wilson nor any administration since has uttered a protesting word on Mexico's brazen breach of the Lansing agreement by a pervasive persecution of religion and a ruthless suppression of human rights paralleled but once in the history of man. This is a broad statement, but the investigation which Senator Borah is demanding, and the administration is busily obstructing, would demonstrate it to readers of history.

U. S. Interventions Powered Persecution

Yet, as these papers have disclosed from incontestable documents, our interferences have been more numerous and effective in favor of the persecutors in Mexico than all our protests against them in other lands. Poinsett, our first envoy, was so interfering, and laying the ground for such future interference, before Webster asserted our right to defend human liberty anywhere. It was our administrations that, by arms and armies, twice thrust into dictatorial power the author of the Juarez Code. This instrument, in its robbing and outlawing of Church and priesthood, presented ample basis for the Constitutions of Carranza and of Calles, who were also empowered to impose them by American assistance.

President Wilson employed army and navy and home and foreign embargoes and sacrificed the privileges of American shipping in the Panama Canal to force Carranza on the Mexican people; and the first Article of the Carranza Constitution is as complete an antithesis of ours as thought or word could make it: "IN THE REPUBLIC OF MEXICO EVERY INDIVIDUAL SHALL HAVE THOSE RIGHTS WHICH ARE GRANTED TO HIM BY THIS CONSTITUTION."

Thus at one stroke does this governing premise dispose of inalienable title to life and liberty or any right whatsoever; and in limiting the people to such rights as a partisan Constitution shall assign them, it makes government and party the origin of right and the arbiter of liberty. Thus was also exemplified the truly American pronouncement of Supreme Court Justice James Wilson, one of the main moulders of our United States Constitution, that the assumption by civil government to prescribe what rights the people shall have is to make civil society the owner of man, and man not the maker but the chattel of society.

Atheizing Children And Shooting Protesters

So it has worked out in Mexico to literal fulfillment. Calles had utilized the powers of this 1917 Constitution to identify his Revolutionary Party with the entire Mexican people and to secure possession of the very consciences of its children and youth, thus reducing all to absolute chattel-dom. The incidental abominations of sacrilege, assassinations, confiscation, expulsion, and outrages of endless variety, have been already outlined or indicated. But the recent order of the Secretary of State that the children shall everywhere be gathered into Sunday services to decry God and religion and glorify the Atheo-Socialist blasphemies, and that a Socialist Congress of children shall be convened in the Capital for the further conquest of consciences, presents perhaps the most striking and vivid picture of the tyranny that is now enslaving the very soul of Mexico.

Its worse than barbaric ruthlessness was exemplified March 1 at Puebla by the brutal assault of soldiery and police upon three thousand men, women and children while marching in peaceful procession to the governor's palace to protest against their atheizing schools. An equally murderous attack on a still larger procession of like protest occurred March 3 at Guadalajara. The hundreds of these ladies, gentle and simple, and their bleeding children that lay wounded or dying will best illustrate, as similar savageries in Mexico City and other cities have already illustrated, the indescribable brutalities which this government feels free to perpetrate in exterminating religion and liberty.

Remove Index Of Our Aid To Tyranny

It is we that have furnished them this freedom. Mr. Dwight Morrow and Mr. Pierpont Morgan made overtures in 1927 and 1928 for cessation of religious persecution in order to provide requisite economic security to American bankers; and they secured a temporary lull. But never once to this hour have our United States administrations intervened to restrain or halt the assault on the religious liberty even of our own nationals in Mexico. The Mexican independent journal, "Excelsior," records February 24, that whereas Ministers Murray of England and Goiran of France had entered protest with the Mexican government against the imposition of the educational amendment on the French and the Franco-English schools, Ambassador Daniels, when requested by the American colony to take like action in favor of an American school, declared that his government's policy (criterio) withheld him from making any protest whatsoever.

A few individuals who rate personal friendship above Mexico's woes or their country's honor, have essayed to defend Mr. Daniels' intervention in support of the Calles personnel and program, on the Machiavelian principle that an ambassador must ingratiate himself with the governing parties no matter how, and that, if we effect the recall of this pious Methodist, his southern coreligionists, though also under Mexican ban, will rise up to overwhelm us. That imaginary risk could be ventured; but it is no question whatsoever of Mr. Daniels' person or character, however estimable.

It is solely a question of the United States government, which his actions have represented, and have been taken by each of the opposing parties to represent, as extending its favor and sanction to the Mexican government in its persecuting policies. His recall has been urged only because this would be the obvious indication to the Mexican people that the United States government does not sanction such policies. If this were made clear by some other method, Mr. Daniels would concern us no further; but until his actions shall be authoritatively repudiated, it will be our patriotic duty as American citizens to demand that this standing sign and symbol of our government's favor to the persecution and persecutors of human liberties in Mexico shall be removed.

CHAPTER XI

SHALL WE KEEP MEXICO A COMMUNIST NURSERY?

Our Right And Duty To Protest

WE have had no qualms about intervening in Mexico's internal affairs when our material interests were involved. These were so precious that Secretary Kellogg set up an embargo to defend them, and President Coolidge declared that intrusion on our soil and mining properties was not a subject of arbitration, being a grave violation of inalienable rights. Even Mr. Daniels has maintained this tradition, having recently entered protest against the confiscation of the Las Rusias lands owned by American citizens. But he has entered no protest, and apparently holds himself inhibited from entering protest, even for his own nationals, against the forfeiture of rights intrinsically sacred and incontestably inalienable.

To vindicate the fundamental right to serve and worship God according to one's conscience, our State Departments and Presidents have freely proffered their good offices not only for our own nationals, but for aliens in lands afar; and we have even conditioned our hapless recognition of Soviet Russia on guarantees of such liberties for American residents therein. Why is it that Mexico, the country on our own border that shares with the Soviets the bad pre-eminence of persecution among the nations of the world, is the one land that hears no word of protest from the Government of the United States?

It is the pressing duty of every patriotic citizen to demand a full and frank answer to that question. It is a further duty to insist that our government shall not obstruct but shall help and hasten congressional inquiry into the religious and other discriminations on our border. It is no longer a question of partial or intermittent oppression of race or creed or denomination. It is a campaign, persistent and relentless, to extinguish Religion itself, and every right and principle that religion compasses. Our fathers appealed to "Nature's God" and "The Creator," by Whom they had been "endowed with inalienable rights." The Committee of Investigation will find that the Mexican persecutors do, by profession and propaganda and constitutional practice, repudiate God and Creator and all rights derived from Him, and that theirs is precisely a war against God, a war that assails and aims to undermine the foundations of civil society.

The Communist Fire Next Door

It is no longer a Catholic or Christian question, nor merely a religious question. It is a fundamental American question. It is a question whether Soviet Communism shall reign in Mexico, and whether, having driven out God and the human rights He implanted, it shall extend its liberty-killing tentacles across our own border. They would seemingly find receptive soil of our own culturing. Our recognition of Soviet Russia, securing its admission to the League of Nations, has facilitated Communist propaganda throughout the world, and particularly here, with no compensatory benefit. Conventions both of Labor and of Commerce and Banking have trumpeted the dangers of its inroads, and the Washington **Star** has presented documented exposures of its perverting activities among our sailors and soldiers and army and navy employes.

The menace seems even deeper and more nearly related to our Mexican policies. Considerable proof emerges for the recent statement of Congressman Fish that our leading universities "are honeycombed with near-communists and communists teaching class hatred, hatred of religion, and hatred of American institutions," and that the inter-collegiate "League of Industrial Democracy" is a hotbed of Communist propaganda. Observers abroad as well as here readily agree that "Communism reaches into every sphere of human activity," that "its destructive web entangles all nations," and that "no country nor people can afford to ignore its menace to civilization"; but another statement made by Congressman Fish in the shadow of the White House demands careful weighing: "There are Socialists, left wing Socialists, near Communists, and Communist sympathizers in Federal service here, appointed by the President and holding important and often key postions."

U. S. Officials Charged With Communist Tinge

Akin to this is the charge of Father Coughlin, February 10, that the charter of the "Public Works Emergency Leasing Corporation," of which Secretary of the Interior Ickes is chief incorporator, contains articles as Communist in theory as "the economic laws or edicts which have emanated from Moscow since 1917." It happens that the chief of the important "Division of Territories and Island Possessions" in the department of Secretary Ickes, Mr. Ernest Gruening, has recently expressed the same trend in the political domain. Reviewing in **The Nation** of January 9, Carleton Beals' "Fire on the Andes," Mr. Gruening agrees with Mr. Beals that the one hope of Peru's escape from her corrupt ruling class, including "rapacious priests," is the establishment of a native Communist republic based on the pagan culture of the Incas. Noting Mr. Beals' apprehension that the anti-Catholic leader, Haya de la Torre, whose anti-religious program is identical with Moscow's, is not collectivist nor communist enough, Mr. Gruening draws comfort from the likelihood that Haya's present restraint is but a matter of expediency.

Mr. Gruening and Mr. Beals have both written books on Mexico, and while they condemn infringements on personal liberty, they stand firmly with the Mexican government against the Church, and they favor in Mexico as in Peru a native communist state that will discard Christian culture for collectivist Indian paganism. Mr. Gruening entertains just such theories as now direct the government of Mexico; and he holds a key position in the administration. Do other parlor Socialists of Communist trend also hold key positions in our government? Would this explain in part Mr. Daniels' escape from censure for his consistent favoring of the Communist rule and rulers of Mexico?

It is of vital importance to the American people, and also to their government's administration, that the investigation demanded by Senator Borah shall be made, and shall furnish answer to these questions.

Resolutions Of Congress And States

The resolutions and expositions of Representatives Fenerty, Celler, Fish, Higgins, and of other able proponents in both Houses, synthesize clearly the protests that have been flowing in rising surge into Congress and Senate and State Department and White House from every section of the country and from every element of our population. Their substance and trend are summarized in the Borah Resolutions, which crystalize the sentiments and express the mind and purpose of the American people. The conclusions flow from comprehensive and well grounded premises:

1. The persecutions of Christians of all faiths in Mexico have aroused indignant protest throughout the world.

2. The outrages have assailed the faiths and homes and civil rights and even lives of American citizens in Mexico.

3. The vindictive anti-religious policy of the Mexican government has so restricted the numbers of clergymen of all creeds and their ministrations as to rescind the people's right to profess and practice the religion of their choosing.

4. The present Mexican government, in accord with the national policy of the dominant Revolutionary Party to obliterate religious worship, prohibits private religious instruction and edu-

cation of children and compels parents to send
their children to schools that teach hatred of
religion, thereby manifesting an anti-religious
activity contrary to the traditions of freedom of
conscience and religious worship, the cherished
attributes of all civilized governments.

5. This government has even promoted an economic boycott against those who profess and
practice the Christian religion, and flagrantly
mistreats and abuses the Christian residents of
Mexico who complain of such intolerance.

6. The distinguished leaders of the Catholic,
Protestant and Jewish faiths and numerous outstanding organizations and societies of the
United States have registered emphatic protest
against such principles and practices.

This is a good but moderate summing of the
case. Among the American protests could now
be included the joint resolutions of the legislatures of Illinois, of North Dakota, of Maryland,
of Massachusetts, of New York, and particularly
of Arizona, which, by a practically unanimous
concurrent memorial, has demanded the adoption of the Borah Resolution in view of the communistic menace on its borders, and notes the
solidarity of Protestants, Catholics, and Jews in
support of this demand.

The resolutions from the Borah premises: that
the United States Senate enter protest against
the anti-religious campaign of ruthless persecution by the present rulers of Mexico and its accompanying brutalities inflicted even upon our
own nationals for the profession and practice of
religion, and that our government demand that
the government of Mexico shall cease to deny

inalienable rights to our citizens domiciled therein, reach fitting climax in the final clause:

"That the Committee on Foreign Relations of the United States Senate, or a subcommittee thereof, be authorized to conduct hearings and receive such evidence as may be presented relating to religious persecution and anti-religious compulsion and agitation in Mexico for the purpose of determining the policy of the United States in reference to this vital problem and in what way we may best serve the cause of tolerance and religious freedom."

Senator Borah wisely refrains from suggesting what course shall be taken until the Senate shall have before it all the authenticated facts to determine its action; but what this should be is indicated by the resolution of the Knights of Columbus and of many other protesting bodies, namely: that unless the present persecutions shall be altogether ended and civil and religious liberty established on a constitutional basis, the United States government shall cut off all friendly relation with the government of Mexico.

The Calles-Communist Gang Must Go

Even this will not suffice. As Archbishop Diaz stated in 1927, and as their immediate and total infraction of the 1929 compact and his own recent lawless and brutal arrest have since amply confirmed, we can place no reliance on word or covenant of these irresponsible tyrants. They will change their constitution and will make any pledge that necessity compels or expediency suggests; but they will not change their spots. They are Soviet Communist to the core; and they will give guarantees, as Stalin gave them, to gain the prestige and manifold advantage of American recognition. But they will belie them as did he; and they will break every pledge and promise, as they have broken them before to their own people and to us.

Realizing that religious minded people will not tolerate their rule, they would eradicate religious and moral principle to maintain themselves in power and pelf; and, obsessed with the atheistic madness and anti-moral determinism of Moscow, they hold no basic principles in common with us. Hence, as Archbishop Diaz said from intimate knowledge, "any compromise with them bears the germ of corruption"; and satisfactory and trustworthy settlement must be made, not with the sworn enemies but with the friends and defenders of civic and religious liberty in Mexico.

The most noted Jewish and Protestant leaders have condemned this "Major Scandal of the World" in the public press and before huge audiences from New York to San Francisco; and the Cardinal Archbishop of Philadelphia, the Archbishops of Baltimore and Portland and San Antonio, the Bishops of Detroit and Los Angeles and Springfield and El Paso, and other prelates of commanding influence, have denounced it by voice and pen and pointed out the government's duty to take action and the people's duty to compel it.

Societies of million memberships are publicizing from coast to coast, that, because of our Administration's countenance of the scandal and its makers, it is eminently also a United States scandal; and they are urging their members with marked success to make protest to their Representatives that it must be ended. These protests, which have mounted into the millions and show no sign of abatement, are also demanding the adoption of the Borah Resolutions.

One ground of their urgings is that presented by the Archbishop of Baltimore; "No better service could be rendered the Governments of the United States and Mexico than to eliminate the sources of misunderstanding and irritation which, like a festering wound, have been developing in the relations of these two countries."

Why Administration Halts Remedial Action?

Why then does the State Department oppose investigation into this Mexico-American scandal? The Secretary's objection, that this was exclusively within the jurisdiction of the President, was overruled by the Foreign Relations Committee, in the parallel Tinkham Resolution to withdraw recognition of Russia, and ran counter to Senatorial usage; and only a year ago Secretary Hull himself set Senator Robinson to denounce in the Senate the persecution of Jews in Germany. A resolution demanding precisely the same kind of information about outrages on the Jews of Ukrainia, which was reported unanimously to the Senate in 1919, was one among several disproofs of the Secretary's claim that the Borah Resolution lacks precedent. He could find it complete in the two Congressional volumes recording actual Resolutions in 1919 and Report in 1920 of "Investigation of Mexican Affairs."

His further claim, that the State Department had no evidence of Mexican violations of Ameri-

can rights, was met by some hundred instances
of flagrant outrages on the properties and persons, the educational and religious rights, and
even on the lives of American citizens, some of
which are noted by Father Thorning in **America**
of March 16. Hence we may well ask with
Archbishop Curley: "What is there so holy and
sacred about the Bolshevik regime in Mexico
that we can fill the air with protests about persecutions in Germany but cannot get a hearing
for those who are being persecuted in Mexico?"

What, then, are the grounds for the Secretary's opposition to Congressional investigation?

These would be, that the State Department
fears investigation into its own dealings with
the persecuting rulers of Mexico; which would
show that Mr. Daniels' laudations of Calles and
Co. and of their official mouthpiece, **El Nacional,**
and of their dereligionizing educational
system, are, as he said of his refusal to protest
in favor of an American school, "in accordance
with his government's policy". That policy's
persistence in refusing to reprove or recall him,
despite manifold evidence that the Mexican
people deem his procedure clear proof of the
United States support of the tyranny that crush-
es them and despite the overwhelming protests
of our own people in their favor, would show
that our Ambassador is but the instrument of
the department he represents and that the party
responsible is the Administration itself.

To Archbishop Curley's question, why investigate persecutions in Germany but not at all in
Mexico, **America,** March 2, gives this answer:

"It is because we did not put the Hitler regime in power in Germany and we did not keep it there. We did put the Calles-Obregon-Cardenas crowd of exploiters in power in Mexico and we have kept them there. An inquiry into religious persecution in Mexico is an inquiry into our own dealings with Mexico. It is not surprising that the State Department does not want any such thing. But is that any reason why its desires should be respected by the Senate? The open resistance by the State Department to an inquiry is the very reason why there should be one. If the Senate is seeking an 'American angle' for the inquiry . . . right here at home lies the real field for investigation: Just how far is our American policy responsible for the growing irritation between Americans and Mexicans over the religious persecution in Mexico and for the threat to the good neighbor policy as it regards the rest of Latin America?"

Lying Propaganda and Special Interests

Other elements darken the issue. Cardinal Dougherty told an audience of forty thousand protesters in Philadelphia that Soviet Russia had contributed millions of dollars to Sovietize Mexico. He could have added that Mexico has spent larger millions in the United States, directly in lying propaganda, and indirectly but more effectively in securing from our journals a concert of silence on its Communist system and its outrages on civilization.

It has turned its U. S. consulates into bureaus of lying propaganda, and it has besides not a few of our clever journalists and legal experts in its pay. When it expelled Archbishop Caruana, the Apostolic Delegate, it had a group of disreputable but able lawyers in New York to defend its action on the basis of a forged entrance signature, which represented the Archbishop as signing himself "Protestant". They publicized this so ingeniously and widely that the general public, including not a few Catholics, believed it; and our government overlooked this double outrage on one of its own most distinguished nationals.

These and other agencies in Washington and elsewhere are now issuing and distributing multiform versions of the blatant Cardenas and Portes Gil mendacities to the gullible, and the New York consul general is broadcasting them over a national radio network. Though these are not now so effective in the present wider understanding of the obvious facts, they have their influence on the Administration's attitude.

There are also state questions involved which have not been submitted to either Congress or people. One of these is the acquisition of a naval base on Magdalena Bay and the lease or cession of Lower California, the peninsula on which it is situated. It was refusal to renew the lease on Magdalena Bay that precipitated the downfall of Porfirio Diaz; and their friendliness or unfriendliness to our occupation of this naval base was a principal factor in the rise or fall or maintenance of subsequent factions. The general patriotic opposition to further "Yanqui" occupation of Mexican territory makes open concession of bay or peninsula impolitic; but Calles has known how to satisfy our government without offending Mexican susceptibilities. In his recent

planting of a Mexican colony in Lower California
to cultivate this hitherto neglected territory, Cardenas threatens to jeopardize our projects.

We Need Reliable Rulers in Mexico

There are sound reasons for this persistent
United States policy. We need that most adequate naval base in view of possible or prob-
able Japanese aggression; and for Mexico this
territory has been and promises to remain a
wilderness. It is therefore highly desirable that
we have a strong and reliable government to
deal with, composed of men on whose wisdom
and word we could depend to establish a permanent settlement in the interest of both peoples;
a truly consitutional government of sane and
honest administrators who would enter into
friendly alliance with the United States for the
protection of American civilization.

The responsible leaders of the movement now
forming against Calles' tyranny are men of such
character; and they would gladly enter into such
an alliance, nor would they fear to do it in the
open. Already authorized Japanese emissaries
have approached them and offered them support;
and this they decisively rejected. These are the
men we should cultivate in the vital and paramount interest of the United States, and no longer demean ourselves by making undisclosable
bargains through clandestine methods and underground channels with untrustworthy and irresponsible tyrants, whose thoughts and ways
and purposes are foreign and abhorent to ours.

Thus we shall, at the same time, have safe-
guarded the nation's interest and executed the

nation's will. It will involve a change of policy; but a change precisely corresponding to the New Deal, by which President Roosevelt has had the courage and statesmanship to reverse long established economic policies in the interest of social justice and human rights. These constitutional as well as natural rights had been filched from the many for the enrichment and supremacy of the few. This is the process that has been operating in Mexico for a century, but more heinously and hurtfully; and never so ruinously as now.

Apply New Deal to Our Mexican Relations

This is also what our United States Administrations have been sponsoring directly and indirectly, positively and negatively, through the whole history of what they call the Mexican Republic. That not one of those Radical, or Socialist, or Communist, but always religion-hating, predatory oligarchies, could have subsisted without our aid or persisted without our sanction, has, we submit, been demonstrated by fact and reference. This narrative has also made manifest that the government which our State Department is now holding to its official heart in diplomatic embrace, is the most formally Communist in purpose and practice, the most brutally and comprehensively oppressive, the most predatory, not only of property and of civil and religious rights, but of conscience itself and of the very children's communion with their God, that has ever dishonored this hemisphere. It is the antithesis of ours in its concept and its workings; and the waves and winds of Communism that are now flooding the world with its poisons render this Soviet pioneer on our borders a menace to ourselves and to our whole governing system. It is Moscow's footprint on the Rio Grande.

Why then do we tolerate it? Why do we still cultivate it? Why do we not extend our New Deal to our foreign diplomacy and instruct our ambassadors to champion within their sphere the forgotten or outraged rights of the common man, whether he be priest or peon or American resident in Mexico? This we have done repeatedly for natives as well as our own nationals in many faraway lands, where in not a single instance were the wrongs protested as destructive of human rights as the Mexican outrages against nature and nature's God. That this charge is literally true will further appear from secret documents issued by the supreme authorities of Mexico. Our citations are from photostats of the originals.

Official Orders To Kill And Corrupt.

One is a "Secret Circular of the Socialist Order'" by the "Permanent Commission of the Congress of the United States of Mexico," which is sent to all the state legislatures and administrative bodies. The legislators are "in no way to molest the Communist elements of the Third International of Moscow, since our Revolutionary Government is holding conference with Joseph Stalin for the renewal of intercourse and diplomatic, commercial and ideological treaties with Russia, the great Soviet Fatherland of the Workers of the World." The State officials are further instructed to make such division of lands of every kind and description as would constitute

agrarian Communism undiluted, to exterminate
the Knights of Columbus and leading Catholics
everywhere, thus "defending the sacrosanct
rights of the Revolution and banishing the whole
clerical gang." The legislatures are finally told
to take note that this Permanent Commission of
Congress will remove executives who are luke-
warm in obeying these orders.

Another secret circular of the same date from
the "United States of Mexico" supplements this
proof of determined warfare against nature and
nature's God. It is addressed to the "Senor Senators" by authority of Carlos Riva Palacios, President of the P. N. R. The Senators are informed
that the best way of completing "the triumph of
the Dictatorship" is a systematic attack on the
clerics and the Knights of Columbus and of Guadalupe. The persecution of these elements will
"bind socialization with golden clasps." The common herd of Catholics may be disregarded, for
their socialization will be best effected in the
schools: "The socialist school and the sexual education will be magnificent auxiliaries in prepara-
tion for universal socialization." It adds that other
organizations have carefully localized the Knights
of Columbus throughout the whole federative entity, "and in due time at a given moment we shall
be able to seize and wipe them out to a man."

Thus the Mexcan government was planning to
maintain its hold by dereligionizing and corrupting systematically the children and youth of Mexico, and by slaughtering those of its citizens who
would preserve the inalienable rights to life, liberty, and the pursuit of happiness conferred on
them by nature and nature's God. Thus also the

United States government, whose constitution and laws are built on these principles, is presented as cooperating in friendliest fashion with the powers that are uprooting them in Mexico; while, as if to confirm this presentation, our Administration sets its face persistently against Congressional investigation into these facts of inhuman tyranny, even when they affect our own nationals.

Catholic, Protestant, Jew Urge U. S. Action

It is high honor to the Knights of Columbus that such a tyranny has doomed them to destruction for maintaining American principles in Mexico; and it is equally to their credit here that they are foremost in maintaining American principles at home and bringing their influence so to bear that our Administration shall apply and maintain them in its relations abroad. They have learned from the mistakes of the past. They see more clearly now than in 1926-1927 that the Mexican question is a question not merely of religion, but of all fundamental rights, and is essentially an American problem which must be settled openly by Congressional authority and not by private agreements with this or that diplomat.

In promoting the Borah Resolution, and in appealing to our people throughout the nation, to Americans of every creed and party, to see to it that their government's Administration shall act in American fashion and stop the destruction of human rights in Mexico or withdraw its friendly hand from the destroyers, the Knights of Columbus are rendering signal services to their country. It is not the least, that they are warding off the Communist peril, which is seeping in from every quarter, but most from its living center across the Rio Grande.

In "The Mexican Crisis," published 1927, this writer considered that the then Knights of Columbus campaign for justice in our relations with Mexico would bring about a civil resurgence and a consciousness of civic power and duty that would render the Catholic body a permanent and unified force of defense and offense in every national need. That opportunity was lost; but the Knights of Columbus are now in the direct way of rendering this service to the nation. And they do not stand alone.

Societies and organizations, preachers and publicists, journals and magazines of every class and creed and party, have protested against the war on religion in Mexico and the brutal persecution of human rights, to an extent unprecedented in our history. Jewish leaders have been prominent in denouncing these outrages from press and platform; and in their stout defense of their own persecuted brethren, our American Catholic body can well find a model for its activities.

Jews Win Rights for Brethren Oppressed

The majority of the many instances cited by Congressman Celler of our government's intervention with foreign governments were in behalf of persecuted Jews; and in nearly every case their cause was pressed until redress was secured. This is highly to the credit of the Jews in the United States, who, though relatively small in number, had the courage and the resourcefulness to put and maintain such pressure on our Administration that they brought the whole force of our government to bear in freeing their alien brethren in distant continents from oppression. In those and other lands there were also Catholics oppressed, but not one of the interventions cited was in their behalf. This was doubtless because, or at least mainly because, our people lacked the civic courage or the unified purpose of their Jewish brethren to demand and insist that this government, which more than twenty million Catholics help to make and function, use also its friendly offices in behalf of Catholics oppressed.

Nor is our present demand made in behalf of Catholics as such; nor is it for victims far away. It is in behalf of a people at our doors more cruelly robbed of all rights, human and divine, than were ever Jews or Christians in the Orient. It is a demand that should never have to be made; for our government, in common justice and in its own interest, should of its own volition have anticipated it. And our first demand is, not that it shall intervene against the oppressors, but that it shall cease intervening in their favor.

A Fight That Must Not Fail

Meanwhile we insist that such an investigation shall be made of the Mexican laws and acts oppressive of all liberties, and of their damaging incidence on American interests, as will enable us to determine whether to cut off connections with such a pervert government in Mexico and favor the defenders of her liberties. It is a fight that must not fail.

Two hundred and fifty Congressmen, a clear majority, presented June 29 and July 10, 1935, an insistent demand to the Secretary of State for prompt remedial and reparative action towards Mexico. If our people by insistent and persistent demand and protest, rally unitedly to the support of these true representatives, they will not fail. Their fight will be a victory for American justice and American honor.

In proposing a New Deal of social justice for the economically oppressed and for the impoverished millions in our own land, President Roosevelt has bravely turned from the false traditions of economic oppression; and he has frequently emphasized the paramount importance of religious principles and a spiritual viewpoint. It cannot therefore be conceived that he wants to maintain the false traditions by which our Administrations have upheld in Mexico the hands not only of economic and political oppression, but the hands that are tearing out every religious principle, every religious ideal, from the heart of the nation, and striving madly to destroy them even at their source.

Communism, or God and Liberty, on Crossway

President Roosevelt appeals to God. The slogan of the Mexican rule and rulers, and their teaching, is: "No Hay Dios," ("There is no God.") Surely he will see that support or countenance for that slogan on one side of the Rio Grande, must forfeit him the Divine support requisite to consummate happily the New Deal upon the other side. Rather would it bring Communism and its poisons. The Knights of Columbus, and the associated bodies of all creeds and classes that are defending the New Deal of governmental justice in the handling of our Mexican problem, must not falter in their insistence that our Representatives in Washington shall respond to the voice of our great Declaration, the voice of our best traditions, the voice of the American people.

It is the cry of human rights and human liberties on the crossways of civilization. It is a question of the new order, or of the new disorder; and for us the Crossway for either is now the Rio Grande. For the sake of our country and of Christian Civilization, it is the imperative duty, at this critical hour, of the Knights of Columbus and of their fellow proponents of human rights throughout this nation, to persist in insisting, and to exact, that our government shall make the Rio Grande the Crossway for right order and Christian liberty between these United States and all the States and all the people of Mexico.

Extract from Statement of the Administrative Committee of the American Hierarchy, May 1, 1934

"The present Revolutionary Government of Mexico was recognized by the United States— October 19, 1915—on condition, and on Mexico's own given word, that freedom of religious worship would be guaranteed to her own citizens.

"We ask that our Government be consistent and live up to its own set policy. We ask our Government to defend before its own people the principles upon which our Government is founded. The traditional policy of our Government does not permit it to remain silent at the present moment and in the present crisis. We may not interfere with the internal affairs of another nation. But freedom of conscience, freedom of religious worship, freedom of education, are principles on which, even for the sake of the least gifted of humanity, our Government was never silent. Good will to neighboring nations means good will to the peoples and the rights of those peoples, as well as to the particular administration that is ruling them. Persecution does not cease to be persecution when invested with the dignity of constitutional or statute law.

"We know, as all the world knows, that an entrenched minority can hold and control an enormous population. Such is the condition that rules today in Mexico. The great majority of its people is practically held in captivity by its government.

"We, the Administrative Committee, National Catholic Welfare Conference, will further spread the knowledge of the facts with regard to Mexico at the present time. We will continue to urge our people to express individually and corporately their petition to our Government that, in the role of the good neighbor, it use its good offices with the Mexican Government to restore religious liberty to its fifteen million citizens."

POSTSCRIPT TO SECOND EDITION.

It should be noted that persecution is even more deadly now than under the grinding rule of Calles. The new faction has but made the uprooting of religion more drastic and inescapable. The Students' revolt prevented the imposition of Atheizing education on the Universities.

This, Cardenas has nullified by withholding all federal funds until they shall accept it. He has done worse. Calles had extended the expropriations to the state of Church properties of every description. Cardenas has just issued a decree proclaiming that every building, house, home or place where any service has been held or instructions given relating in any way to religion or cult, or where any priest or minister has resided, becomes thereby the property of the state. Moreover, no legal proof is needed to justify such confiscation. Presumption of religious uses is sufficient; and Cardenas offers state reward to any who will supply grounds for the presumption.

This diabolic device, striking at once at Priests and laymen and enriching grafters and traitors, is the most killing blow to religion that has yet been struck. Over two thousand priests are hiding in Mexico, offering Mass in friendly homes and serving stealthily their people. With this decree enforced, to offer Mass or accept refuge in a home is to ask one's host to risk confiscation of house and goods and the persecution and ruin of his family. It thus shuts out priests and Mass and Christian teaching more effectually than decrees of exile or death. Humanly speaking it will soon have made literally true the title of this book, unless we of the United States take effective action to Keep God next door and to save our Mexican brethren from religious destruction.